Twayne's United States Authors Series

Sylvia E. Bowman, *Editor*

INDIANA UNIVERSITY

John G. Neihardt

TUSAS 270

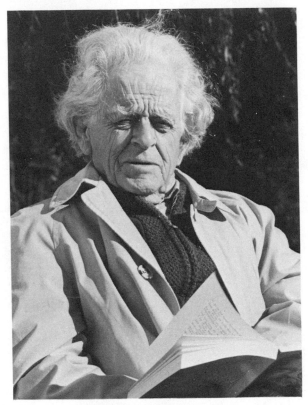

John G. Neihardt

JOHN G. NEIHARDT

By BLAIR WHITNEY

Illinois Board of Higher Education

TWAYNE PUBLISHERS

A DIVISION OF G. K. HALL & CO., BOSTON

Library of Congress Cataloging in Publication Data

Whitney, Blair.
    John G. Neihardt.

    (Twayne's United States authors series ; TUSAS
270)
    Bibliography: p. 155 - 57.
    Includes index.
    1.   Neihardt, John Gneisenau, 1881-1973.
PS3527.E35Z95   811'.5'2 [B]   76-6543
ISBN 0-8057-7170-0

MANUFACTURED IN THE UNITED STATES OF AMERICA

To my Mother and Father

Contents

About the Author

Blair Whitney, like John Neihardt, is a Midwesterner. Reared in Springfield, Illinois, he received B.A., M.A., and Ph.D. degrees from the University of Illinois. He has taught at Illinois, Central Missouri State University, and Michigan State University, and is presently Staff Associate for Academic Affairs for the Illinois Board of Higher Education.

Dr. Whitney has published articles on American literature in a variety of scholarly journals and has delivered papers at several national professional meetings. He is also active in the Society for the Study of Midwestern Literature.

Preface

On November 4, 1973, John G. Neihardt died at the age of ninety-two. At the time of his death, he was preparing the second volume of his autobiography. Although his hearing and eyesight weakened near the end, he retained much of the physical and intellectual vigor that sustained him over a seventy-five-year writing career. This book is the first comprehensive study of his entire work; beginning with a discussion of his life and literary creed, this study deals, in order, with his lyric poetry, verse plays, prose fiction, and history; and it concludes with a thorough discussion of his blank-verse epic *A Cycle of the West*.

Neihardt's lyric poetry, most of which was written before his thirtieth year, is uneven in quality, although it received high praise when it first appeared. The lyrics of "A Poet's Town," however, are less personal, more socially concerned than his other short poems, and also more likely to endure. Neihardt's prose fiction, most of which was also written before 1912, is often excellent. The early stories about fur trappers and Indians give the reader insight into the character of men under stress. The early novels are failures; but *When the Tree Flowered*, written late in Neihardt's career, is a masterful fictional treatment of the Sioux nation from the era of its prime through its tragic fall and then to the present day.

Perhaps Neihardt's best writing occurs in his nonfiction, which he also used to provide historical background for his epic. *The Splendid Wayfaring* is about Jed Smith's heroic explorations and is also a profound character study of that remarkable figure. *Black Elk Speaks*, Neihardt's most popular work, is recognized as one of the best books ever written about the American Indian. Most critics, from its publication to the present day, have praised it as literary art of the highest order. Neihardt's epic, *A Cycle of the West*, took thirty years of intense labor to complete, and while it is not completely successful as a whole, it does contain many individual sections of excellent poetry.

In spite of his long and productive career, Neihardt's work has never received the critical attention and critical praise it deserves. This study is intended as a first step in a much-needed critical reappraisal. It is also an attempt to demonstrate the tremendous vitality of both the man and his work. I have quoted often and at some length from Neihardt's work in order to demonstrate not only his achievements but also those moments when his epic reach is not quite equal to his grasp. These critical judgments are entirely my own responsibility; but my hope is that this book will encourage its readers to buy Neihardt's books, give them the careful reading they deserve, and then make up their own ninds about this important writer.

Dr. Neihardt and his daughter, Mrs. Hilda Petri, have generously granted me permission to quote from his works. I can only hope to repay this kindness by bringing him some new readers. The research for this book was partially supported by a University Research Grant from Michigan State University. Finally, this study could not have been completed without the patience and tolerance of my wife and children.

BLAIR WHITNEY

Illinois Board of Higher Education

Acknowledgments

I am grateful to Dr. Neihardt and Mrs. Hilda Petri for permission to quote from his works and to Harcourt Brace Jovanovich, Inc. for permission to quote from *All Is But a Beginning*.

Chronology

1925   *The Song of the Indian Wars* (epic); *Poetic Values: Their Reality and Our Need of Them* (criticism).

1926 - Literary editor, St. Louis *Post Dispatch*.
1938

1926   *Collected Poems, Indian Tales and Others.*

1932   *Black Elk Speaks* published, later translated into eight languages.

1935   *The Song of the Messiah* (epic).

1941   *The Song of Jed Smith* (epic).

1949 - Poet-in-residence and lecturer in English, University of
1961   Missouri.

1949   *A Cycle of the West* published in historical sequence.

1951   *When the Tree Flowered* (novel).

1961   First Sunday in August named annual Neihardt Day in Nebraska by governor's proclamation.

1972   *All Is But a Beginning* (autobiography).

1973   Dies November 4, while writing second volume of his autobiography.

CHAPTER 1

A Poet's Life

JOHN G. Neihardt found a way to live a unified, organic, transcendental life in the twentieth century; and his success might serve as an excellent example for anyone trying to live the life of the mind in a troubled and confused age. In *Black Elk Speaks*, *When the Tree Flowered*, *The Song of the Indian Wars*, and other works, Neihardt describes how the sacred hoop of the Sioux nation, the symbol of national and spiritual unity, was broken by the white man who slaughtered the buffalo, Maka's gift to the Sioux, and then imprisoned Maka herself, the Mother Earth, with bands of iron. When the hoop was broken, the sacred Tree of Life at its center withered and died, and the Sioux lost their identity as a people. Neihardt, however, was able to preserve the hoop of his own character and to maintain the integrity necessary for his poetic mission.

The word, "mission" may seem a difficult one to accept in this skeptical age, but that is how Neihardt regarded his work. The true poet, he believed, is a visionary bard, a seer, a man who goes to the mountaintop and brings back a message for his people. Neihardt remained true to this vocation from his adolescence; and, when he was in his nineties, the voice of Little Bull Buffalo, as his Omaha friends called him, was still strong. When he appeared on a nationally televised talkshow, the epitome of superficiality, the contrast between his personal integrity and the surroundings in which he appeared provided a perfect metaphor for his entire life. Neihardt had always emphasized the need for poetic values in a materialistic society without ever retreating from that society. Instead of divorcing himself from the mass of men as many other modern poets have done, he maintained a democratic faith in the best possibilities of all men.

I *Poverty and Inspiration*

John Greenleaf (later changed to Gneisenau) Neihardt was born on January 8, 1881, in a rented farmhouse near Sharpsburg, Illinois. He gave an excellent account of that night, as he later imagined it, in his recently published autobiography, *All Is But a Beginning*. He was born on a cold, raw evening in the farmhouse, only a two-room shack, that his mother, Alice Culler Neihardt, had made respectable with curtains cut from newspapers and with a carpet made from a wagon cover stained with green walnut juice. John's sisters, ages two and four, were dressed and waiting for the "welcoming committee," "an old German woman with a featherbed upon her back stumbling along the road in the deepening twilight."[1]

John's father, Nicholas Neihardt, tried a variety of jobs with little success and later deserted the family; but his son always remembered him fondly as a man without schooling who nevertheless talked of Charles Darwin, Thomas Huxley, and Robert G. Ingersoll and who named his son after John Greenleaf Whittier. In *All Is But a Beginning*, Neihardt recalls his good times with his father during the years they lived in Kansas City where Nicholas Neihardt found brief prosperity as a cable-car conductor. When the father took his son to see the Missouri River in flood, the awesome sight triggered something in the boy's imagination: "There was a dreadful fascination about it — the fascination of all huge and irresistible things. I had caught my first wee glimpse into the infinite. I was six years old."[2]

Even more fascinating, however, were the Kansas and Nebraska prairies where Neihardt grew up. Mrs. Neihardt took the children to live with her parents in a one-room sod house. There young John quickly learned of both Nature's beauty and Nature's power to destroy. The children picked buffalo chips for fuel, felt the tooth of Kansas wind blowing across the treeless plain, and witnessed the awesome, terrible beauty of a prairie fire. In spite of the family's poverty, Neihardt recalls: "It was a happy place and time, as I remember it; for Hope, too, grew big in Kansas. A little now was much, for next year would be better. The drouth last year was over, and the corn was doing well. Faith and a little rain — that was all the country needed."[3] These same memories later furnished material for Neihardt's poetry. As he explained in his preface to *A Cycle of the West*, "If I write of hot-winds and grasshoppers, of prairie fires and blizzards, of dawns and noons and sunsets and nights, of brooding heat and thunderstorms in vast lands, I knew them early. They were the vital facts of my world, along with talk of the old-timers who knew such fascinating things to talk about."[4]

The Kansas prairie and the small town of Wayne, Nebraska, where the family later moved, might seem to be poor places for a poet's education, but young John had a remarkably happy childhood. At first he was interested in mechanical things, in elaborate model ships and steam engines for example; but he had an experience in 1892, which awakened his interest in poetry. Seriously ill with a fever, he had a strange dream which kept recurring:

. . . I was flying face downward, with arms and hands thrust forward like a diver's. There was vastness — terribly empty, save for a few lost stars, too dim and wearily remote ever to be reached. And there was dreadful speed, a speed so great that whatever lay beneath me — whether air or ether — turned hard and slick as glass.

I wanted to rest. I wanted to go home. But when I cried out in desperation, it seemed a great Voice filled the hollow vastness and drove me on. There was something dear to leave behind, something yonder to be overtaken. Faster! faster! faster![5]

This dream changed the pattern of Neihardt's life, and he later wrote of it in his lyric "The Ghostly Brother." In this poem, the poet appeals to the force which is driving him onward toward some unknown goal. This force is the "Ghostly Brother" of the title, and the unseen voice of Neihardt's dream:

> I am breathless from the flight
> Through the speed-cleft, awful night!
> Panting, let me rest awhile
> In this pleasant aether-isle.[6]

But the Ghostly Brother did not let the poet rest. Neihardt himself interpreted this poem as a conflict between two desires within the individual: one wants only the usual human satisfactions; another drives him on toward a less personal, more spiritual goal.[7]

For Neihardt, this goal was to be a poet; and he began with characteristic energy and dedication to learn the craft of poetry. After buying a few books, notably Alfred Lord Tennyson's *Idylls of the King*, to serve as models, he began to write, not just simple rhymes, but epics. Each one contained hundreds of lines — *Chalboa* and *Tlingilla*, which had stone-age settings; and *The Wizard of the Wind*, which was inspired by the *Aeneid*. He also composed a

burlesque of a camp-revival meeting entitled *The Tentiad*, which
W. S. Goldie, "the intellectual bad boy" of Wayne, Nebraska,
published in his notorious paper, *Nebraska Democrat*.[8] Neihardt's
early interest in literature and in other arts was encouraged by two
characters who might have stepped out of Edgar Lee Master's *Spoon
River Anthology* or from Sherwood Anderson's *Winesburg, Ohio*.
"Professor" Durrin was a tombstone carver who hired John as a mar-
ble polisher; and Judge James Brittain was a magistrate who loved
William Shakespeare better than William Blackstone.

Young Neihardt's love for the classics, thus nourished, continued
all his life; and he actually felt the direct influence of "the ancients"
on his own life: "But what we call the slow lapse of ages is but the
blinking of an eye. Sometimes this close sense of the unity of all time
and all human experience has come upon me so strongly that I have
felt, for an intense moment, how just a little hurry on my part might
get me there in time to hear Aeschylus training a chorus, or to see the
wizard chisel still busy with the Parthenon frieze, or to hear Socrates
telling his dreams to his judges."[9]

Neihardt read these classics at Nebraska Normal College in
Wayne, which he entered at the age of thirteen. He worked his way
through by ringing the school bell every hour from six-thirty in the
morning until suppertime. By taking advantage of the special classes
established just for him, he earned a bachelor of science degree for
completing the advanced scientific course by the time he was fifteen.
He never possessed his diploma, however, because he lacked the
four-dollar fee charged for it. That summer, while he pulled weeds
in the potato fields for seventy-five cents a day, his coat pockets were
stuffed with the poetry of Tennyson and of Robert Browning; and
his mind was also full of his own poetry.

During this time he composed his first major work, *The Divine
Enchantment* (1900), which a New York firm agreed to publish after
he paid them two hundred dollars. *The Divine Enchantment* is a
long narrative poem inspired by Neihardt's reading of Eastern
philosophy. In the sacred writings of Hinduism, the young poet
found an equivalent for his quest for spiritual understanding. Like
the New England Transcendentalists, he wanted to marry eastern
spirit to Western flesh and to achieve Walt Whitman's metaphorical
"passage to India." Like Thoreau, John Neihardt read almost no
contemporary literature; for he believed that the oldest wisdom was
also the truest. But Neihardt was not successful in his first attempt at
realizing the ideal. In spite of some favorable reviews, most of the
five hundred copies of the first and only edition of *The Divine*

Enchantment ended in his stove; and, until the day of his death, whenever Neihardt found a copy, he bought it, burned it, and called it "the case of posterity against John G. Neihardt."[10]

Teaching in a country school and working in other low-paid jobs followed as Neihardt continued to write, but he turned from writing an epic to writing lyric verse and to trying his hand at selling short stories. One of these early stories, "The Alien," was quite a sensation; and, though many others were published, Neihardt still saw himself primarily as a poet and firmly resolved to make poetry his life's work. As he later explained,

I developed a tremendous ego, but it was a matter of self-preservation. All poets, all who are accomplished by being different, must develop egoism. When I assert myself, boldly praise something I have done, it is never self-love, but self-denial that speaks. Have I not given a life to my work? Could I not get more immediate comfort for less effort? And would I not willingly die a pauper if I could thereby further my work? My assertion, that may disgust the unwise, is merely by way of accelerating my dynamo, so that the work may not fail. It is a weapon hurled at *momentary doubt*. Deep down I am humble enough, but only to what I conceive to be the enduring values.[11]

But even poets must eat; and, to pay his bills, Neihardt took up journalism. After serving briefly as a reporter on the Omaha *Daily News*, he purchased the Bancroft, Nebraska, *Blade*. He also worked for an Indian trader, and he learned much about the people who were to fill his books. He listened to the old men tell their stories, and the Omaha Indians repaid his respect and courtesy by christening him "Little Bull Buffalo" because of his broad shoulders and his thick mane of yellow hair. Although Neihardt was small, he was strong and vigorous; and he demonstrated his stamina in his long canoe trip down the Missouri River which he describes in *The River and I*. During these years, Neihardt also met old veterans of the Indian Wars; and he encouraged them to relate to him their memories. He was already preparing for his major work.

II   *Building a Reputation*

Meanwhile, his lyrics were circulating in manuscript. His first collection, *A Bundle of Myrrh*, found a New York publisher in 1907; and his literary career was launched. These early poems, some of them quite passionate for their day, found their way to Paris where they were read eagerly by a young sculptor, a student of Auguste Rodin, named Mona Martinsen. Her roots were also in the West because her father had been the president of the Missouri, Kansas, and Texas Railroad. She wrote to Neihardt, and, after a courtship by mail, she traveled to Omaha in 1908. He met her at the station with the marriage license in his pocket, and their marriage lasted until her death in 1958. They had four children, Enid, Sigurd, Hilda, and Alice.

Neihardt's literary output during the first few years of his marriage was prodigious — many poems were collected in *Man Song* (1909) and in *The Stranger at the Gate* (1912); several short stories; four verse plays; and two novels, *Life's Lure* (1914) and *The Dawn Builder* (1911). Most of this work was well received, and he began to build a solid reputation. At thirty-one, secure in his talent, he dedicated himself to *A Cycle of the West*, a labor which was not completed until his sixtieth year. Though he wrote some other verse and prose, notably *Black Elk Speaks*, and a great deal of literary criticism for the St. Louis *Post-Dispatch* and the Minneapolis *Journal* during these twenty-nine years, Neihardt spent every possible moment working on the five epic songs which constitute *A Cycle* — *The Song of Hugh Glass* (1915), *The Song of Three Friends* (1919), *The Song of the Indian Wars* (1925), *The Song of the Messiah* (1935), and *The Song of Jed Smith* (1941).

Neihardt provided for himself and his family by serving as literary editor of the *Post-Dispatch*, by making reading tours around the country, and by teaching. In 1948, he was appointed Poet-in-Residence at the University of Missouri. His readings, which he at first gave only because he needed money, became quite popular because he quickly became a skilled platform performer, although he worried about becoming a "public stunt." He read his epics slowly, with dignity, taking full advantage of their rhythms. According to one listener, "When he reads that the sky 'spat a stinging frost,' he flicks out the sibilants and plosives, and touches the nasal *ng* lightly to give the sense of cold that stings."[12] His audiences, which ranged from teachers and students to cowboys and Indians, were often strongly moved, both by his poetry and by his impressive presence. Once an old rancher came up to him after a recitation and complained, "Damn it, you've made me cry"; and once Neihardt proudly wrote home that Edwin Markham had heard him read and had proclaimed, "I think I have never been more moved than by Neihardt's epic reading. He had done for the prairies what Homer did for Illium."[13] Old Black Elk spoke of his friend as a "word-sender" and named him "Flaming Rainbow" because, in his words, "The world is like a garden. Over this garden go his words like rain, and where they fall they make it a little greener. And when his words have passed, the memory of them will stand long in the west like a flaming rainbow." [14]

Though none of Neihardt's books became best-sellers (*Black Elk Speaks* has now achieved that status forty years after its original publication), and though he has not yet gained entrance into the pantheon of modern poets, he received considerable recognition, especially in his home state of Nebraska. His first honorary doctorate came in 1917 from the university he had been too poor to attend, and his epics were reprinted in school editions so that Nebraska's sons and daughters might better understand their own heritage. In 1921, the state legislature passed a resolution which contradicts all those who accuse Midwesterners of being philistines:

Whereas, John G. Neihardt, a citizen of Nebraska, has written a national epic wherein he has developed the mood of courage with which our pioneers explored and subdued our plains, and thus has inspired in Americans that love of land and its heroes whereby great national traditions are built and perpetuated. . . .
John G. Neihardt be, and hereby is declared poet laureate of Nebraska.[15]

Besides these honors, almost all of Neihardt's books were highly praised by their reviewers, but his name is almost never mentioned in the lists of major American poets, and his work does not appear in the college-teaching anthologies of American literature. There are several reasons for Neihardt's relative obscurity, and one of them is that he refused to succumb to the fleshpots of New York or to an eastern university. Instead, he lived quietly in Lincoln, Nebraska, and on his country place near Columbia, Missouri. While there may not be an "eastern establishment media conspiracy" in literature, the midwestern writer who stays home does have a harder time becoming popular. The fine novelist Wright Morris recently remarked that the midwestern writer lacks the audience that a southern or an urban writer has,[16] and a look at a recent best-seller list proves the truth of his statement.

Another reason for Neihardt's lack of literary fame is that he went against all the trends in contemporary literature. He began his career writing free verse at a time when such a style was new and experimental; but, by the time of World War I, when many poets were writing free verse and proclaiming it to be the only way to liberate poetry from Victorian conventions, Neihardt had already stopped writing it. He had gone back to heroic couplets because he believed that iambic pentameter was the best meter for English verse and that, in fact, it required greater control and greater literary ability to adhere to a rule than to break one. He also realized that a poet could use standard forms and still be experimental; moreover, Neihardt liked the challenge of writing couplets that did not become monotonous, and he liked to see himself as part of the epic tradition from Homer to Tennyson. As a result, he wrote epic poetry at a time when most people no longer read at bedtime a verse tale by Lord Byron, Tennyson's *Idylls*, or even Longfellow's *Hiawatha*, which is infinitely inferior to Neihardt's Indian poems.

Another reason for the lack of appreciation of Neihardt's poetry was that it contrasted to that of the group of poets who dominated American poetry from 1915 or so until quite recently. Though all the major poets were not Imagists, they were almost all strongly influenced by Imagism. Ezra Pound, T. S. Eliot, Amy Lowell, William Carlos Williams, and many others believed that poetry should be concrete, exact, and specific, and that it should use images and symbols to suggest meanings, rather than to state them directly. Any hint of the sentimental was to be avoided; Romanticism was dead; and new subjects needed new poetic forms. This new poetry needed a new kind of literary criticism; and T. S. Eliot, whose poetry became a standard by which all other modern verse was judged, also became the leading critic. He banished most of the Romantics, brought the Metaphysical poets back to popularity, and helped create the New Criticism which dominated both the "little magazines" and university English departments and which determined, therefore, the literary taste of two generations. Those modern poets whose work did not conform to the tastes and to the standards of the New Criticism were, intentionally or unintentionally, banished to literary oblivion.

No poetry is more different, in both form and subject matter from Pound's and Eliot's than that of John G. Neihardt. Eliot called himself a royalist in politics, a classicist in literature, and an Anglo-Catholic in religion. Ezra Pound made propaganda broadcasts for Mussolini. The leading New Critics, while not Fascists, were also conservatives. John Crowe Ransom, Robert Penn Warren, Allen Tate, and Cleanth Brooks were southerners who valued the antebellum grace of pillared mansions and defended a Southern aristocracy against Yankee encroachment. Neihardt, in contrast to these men, was a strong believer in democracy. His religion was not a fashionable Anglo-Catholicism, but a deep faith in the spiritual values of America, those represented by Jed Smith, who carried a Bible into the wilderness, and by Black Elk. The poetry of Pound and Eliot is often densely symbolic, so much so that it requires very intense reading even by well-educated readers who have the necessary background to understand its allusions. Eliot wrote his own footnotes to *The Waste Land,* and they are almost as long as the poem itself. Neihardt's poetry is designed for a wider audience. That does not mean it is easy or simpleminded, or "pop" poetry — for Neihardt despised the Edgar Guests as much as any New Critic — but that it is often a poetry of direct statement. It is not Metaphysical, nor is it good material for the kind of intense *explication de texte* favored by New Critics, but it does repay close reading. It can be read successfully by both Nebraska school children and by university professors.

To the New Critics, a poem should exist in and of itself, apart from history, religion, or philosophy; and they admire chiefly those lyric poems which can be read in that way. Neihardt's poetry, however, cannot be read apart from the history which is its major concern. New Criticism undervalues much Romantic poetry, with the possible exception of that of Keats, because it deals directly with powerful, personal emotions. For Eliot, poetry is not an expression of personality but an escape from it. Neihardt, on the other hand, is the direct heir of nineteenth-century Romanticism. The big Romantic epics of Tennyson, for example, seem to some critics to be inferior to the smallest poem by John Donne because they value complexity and ambiguity. Neihardt's poetry is not the least bit ambiguous.

Finally, Neihardt's entire philosophy of life is in direct conflict with that of most major twentieth-century American writers, novelists, and playwrights as well as poets. Pound, Eliot, Ernest Hemingway, F. Scott Fitzgerald, Eugene O'Neill — these men were all members of the Lost Generation who, in the words of Fitzgerald's character Amory Blaine, had grown up to find "all gods dead, all wars fought, all faiths in man shaken."[17] They had seen the carnage of the Great War and doubted man's ability to save himself. Like Hemingway's Jake Barnes in *The Sun Also Rises,* they were the walking wounded, the casualties in spirit if not in body. They had come home to find normalcy and Babbittry; and the Midwest, where many of them had grown up, was now Main Street or Middletown. Business was God, and Silent Cal was His priest. Disgusted, many writers left for Paris where they learned the teachings of Gertrude Stein and James Joyce. Since democracy seemed not to be working very well, they gave up hope of its ever working. In *Smart Set,* H. L.

Mencken castigated the "booboisie" and developed an elitism which served as a defense against the crass commercialism of American society. Mencken's complaints about Warren Gamaliel and his successors were certainly justified, but in literature this elitism led to a loss of audience and meant surrendering poetry to Edgar A. Guest instead of staying home to fight for a better educated, more appreciative audience. William Carlos Williams was an exception to this rejection of democratic idealism, but his superb poetry did not receive much recognition until after World War II.

This review is not to denigrate in any way the magnificent achievements of these lost generation writers, but these achievements were made at a tremendous cost. Today poetry is read chiefly in universities. Slim volumes of verse rest on the coffee tables of a very few, when they should be stacked high on the shelves of every drugstore. The United States has dozens of good, original poets, but the only poets who sell more than a few thousand copies seem to be the heirs of Eddie Guest — Rod McKuen, for example. Poetic drama has almost disappeared from the contemporary stage, in spite of the heroic efforts of Archibald MacLeish and Robert Lowell.

III   *The Function of Literature*

For all these reasons, John Neihardt was troubled by much of modern literature, although he admired the technical skill of many writers. In the reviews he wrote for the St. Louis *Post-Dispatch*, he often expressed his doubts about the humane value of some modern literature. He called Hemingway's *A Farewell to Arms* "venereal fiction," in spite of its many "vivid and admirable passages." Hemingway's failure, Neihardt believed, was an ethical one. As he explained his view,

. . . it is obvious enough that the purpose of the author was not concerned with the revelation of human life in its larger relations. On the contrary, the obvious purpose is to offer a vicarious satisfaction to those who are either too jaded or too timid to get that satisfaction in a normal way through actual experience. . . . At any rate, the finale is well calculated to arouse self-congratulatory shivers among the confirmed spinsters and should serve as a solemn warning to careless amateurs. But why offend a sophisticated author by intimating that he may be a practical moralist after all? Morality! Horrors! Does he want to lose caste in all the best literary circles?[18]

For Neihardt to admire it, literature had to offer more than a sophisticated picture; it had to provide a vision which increases the reader's understanding. James Joyce, he once wrote in a review, achieves this quality in *Dubliners,* when the stories "burn their way into the consciousness of the reader."[19] The early stories of Sherwood Anderson share this quality, and Neihardt regretted its loss in Anderson's later work in which ". . . the demi-urgic quality is lacking — the synthesizing vision that results in an organic whole."[20] Among younger writers, John Steinbeck has this quality "of seeing clearly and feeling deeply."[21]

To use literature for something other than the expression of the synthesizing vision was, Neihardt believed, to debase it. Although he was a political liberal, he objected to the use of literature as political propaganda, either by the left or by the right; and, in his review of Granville Hicks's *The Great Tradition,* he objects to Hicks's use of political standards for judging works of art.[22] In all Neihardt's criticism, he stands firmly for his concept of the writer as a seer or prophet — as the man who can realize the ideal without idealizing the real. To Neihardt, poetry is something more than a superior entertainment, as Eliot once defined it; it has an important social function because it teaches morals and ethics without preaching. Neihardt was certainly no prude, as his early lyrics clearly prove. In fact, genteel reviewers once assailed him for what they thought were excesses of passion and brutality. He was not afraid to depict the unpleasant side of life; and he depicted it not because he wanted to shock or titillate but because he wanted to write the truth.

Neihardt was born about ten years too soon to be a member of the lost generation. His poetic contemporaries are Edwin Arlington Robinson, Robert Frost, Edgar Lee Masters, and Vachel Lindsay; and his verse is somewhat similar to theirs. Like theirs, his poetry is often elegiac; it mourns the passing of a way of life which was better than that which replaced it. Neihardt thinks of life in the same terms as old Lucinda Matlock in Masters' *Spoon River Anthology.* This hearty, healthy pioneer woman, who is modeled after Masters' own grandmother, lectures her effete descendants in the last lines of the poem:

> What is this I hear of sorrow and weariness,
> Anger, discontent, and drooping hopes?
> Degenerate sons and daughters,
> Life is too strong for you —
> It takes life to love Life.[23]

E. A. Robinson's Tillbury Town, like Masters' Petersburg, was left to decay as cities grew larger and as the frontier moved west. Like Winesburg, Ohio, and dozens of other small towns in American literature, the town's culture is dying, and its citizens are "grotesques." Robinson, however, can still hope for the future: "For through it all — above, beyond it all —/I know the far-sent message of the years,/I feel the coming glory of the Light."[24] Though the United States is now an urban nation, it can still gain strength from the old ways by being versed in the "country things" of Robert Frost.[25] Looking backward is not simple escapism; it is a way of discovering fundamental truths of human nature.

Like Frost and Masters, Vachel Lindsay also tried to reassert older American values against the coming of an urban, industrial age. He dreamed of turning his hometown of Springfield, Illinois, into a utopia where "Lincoln-hearted men" would honor poetry and art. His poems about such Midwestern heroes as Abraham Lincoln, William Jennings Bryan, Jane Addams, John Chapman (Johnny Appleseed), and Mark Twain are attempts to find models for the good life. Lindsay devoted his entire career to preaching his "gospel of beauty," but the audiences at his very popular readings usually mistook him for just another species of entertainer — as a sort of verbal clown. At fifty-one, worn out in both mind and body, and without ever having found the coherent philosophy that allows a poet to continue writing after the original burst of lyric energy has passed, he committed suicide by drinking a bottle of Lysol. The Illinois Legislature then honored him with a resolution; had these gentlemen been as wise as their Nebraska counterparts, who honored Neihardt early, Lindsay might have made it. But pious hopes do not raise dead poets from their graves.

Neihardt outlasted all his contemporaries and most of the following generation as well. The physical vigor of Little Bull Buffalo was equaled, and in his old age was exceeded, by his continued strength of mind and spirit. Though he did not burst upon the literary scene as Lindsay did, though he did not receive immediate recognition with his first book like Frost, he continued to develop his art over a *seventy-five-year* writing career, and he also developed a personal philosophy which gave him remarkable staying power. He found his perfect subject early and worked with constant dedication to perfect his work. By doing so, he fashioned a body of work that seems likely to survive long after some more famous poets are forgotten.

Neihardt's way of seeing things also provided him with an artistic tradition in which to work. He belongs to the "organic tradition" in American art which includes Emerson, Thoreau, Whitman, William Carlos Williams in poetry; John Steinbeck and Frank Waters in the novel; Louis Sullivan and Alfred Steiglitz in photography; the Hudson River School in painting; Frank Lloyd Wright in architecture; and Charles Ives in music. The best definition of what the organic artist believes occurs in a letter from young Louis Sullivan to old Walt Whitman:

CHICAGO, Feb. 3rd, 1887.

My dear and honored Walt Whitman:

It is less than a year ago that I made your acquaintance, so to speak, quite by accident, searching among the shelves of a book store. I was attracted by the curious title: Leaves of Grass, opened the book at random, and my eyes met the lines of Elemental Drifts. You then and there entered my soul, have not departed, and never will depart. . . .

To a man who can resolve himself into subtle unison with Nature and humanity as you have done, who can blend the soul harmoniously with material, who sees good in all and overflows in sympathy toward all good things, enfolding them with his spirit: to such a man I joyfully give the name of Poet — the most precious of all names.[26]

The organic poet is also a Transcendentalist; he works through Nature to Spirit according to Emerson's three-part theory of language:

1. Words are signs of natural facts.
2. Particular natural facts are the signs of particular spiritual facts.
3. Nature is the symbol of spirit.[27]

Whether the organic artist works in words, stone, or paint, he seeks to find the "correspondences," as Emerson called them, between the natural and the spiritual. In *Walden*, for example, Thoreau's pond becomes the earth's eye, "looking into which the beholder measures the depth of his own nature."[28]

By discovering symbols which link the real world with the ideal, the Transcendentalist transcends the ordinary limits of human understanding and can grasp fundamental truths by a kind of spiritual insight. Alfred Steiglitz, for example, took hundreds of pictures of clouds, hoping to find in them exact equivalents to every state of human emotion. Louis Sullivan believed that an architect's most important attribute was not his technical skill but his poetic imagination, and he expressed this imagination in his buildings. A building, he believed, could be like a poem, a symbolic connection between the natural and the spiritual: "So the materials of a building are but the elements of earth removed from the matrix of nature, and reorganized and reshaped by force; by force mechanical, muscular, mental, emotional, moral and spiritual. If these elements are to be robbed of divinity, let them at least become truly human."[29] Charles Ives, perhaps America's greatest composer, had an analogous theory of music, one which he called a "transcendental language."[30]

As the title suggests, the organic artist studies nature and its creative process, which resembles the process by which a work of art is created. In *Walden,* Thoreau tells of a "strong and beautiful bug" that suddenly emerged from an old apple-wood table after it had stood in a farmer's kitchen for sixty years. From this fable Thoreau reasons,

Who knows what beautiful and winged life, whose egg has been buried for ages under many concentric circles of woodenness in the dead dry life of society, deposited at the first in the alburnum of the green and living tree, which has been gradually converted into the semblance of its well-seasoned tomb, — heard perchance gnawing out now for years by the astonished family of man, as they sat round the festive board, — may unexpectedly come forth from amidst society's most trivial and handselled furniture, to enjoy its perfect summer life at last!"[31]

The artist's function is to strip off corrupting influences like layers of dead bark and to find the living tree beneath. This metaphor of the living tree is also central to Neihardt's poetry and provides the title for his last and best novel, *When the Tree Flowered.* The creative artist is of value to society chiefly because he can show it the living tree; he can rekindle the dying fires of creation and restore man's original relationship to the universe, a relationship that he has lost through his own selfishness.

In short, the ideal artist is an awakener. Thoreau writes often in *Walden* of the need to be mentally, spiritually, and morally awake. In the "American Scholar Address," Emerson calls upon Americans to awaken to their own original genius. In his brilliant, but sometimes crusty essays, Charles Ives tries to awaken the public to a new kind of music, to one which will jolt them out of their comfortable assumptions. To be original requires that the artist take chances, experiment, and be willing to fail. He may succeed at first, or it may take a lifetime for him to create a perfect work. Thoreau spent nine years writing *Walden,* and he concludes that awakening book with the fable of the artist of Kouroo who took whole epochs to carve the perfect staff. Ordinary time is an illusion for such an artist, only the stream he goes afishing in; and the true artist willingly sacrifices for his art. John Neihardt spent twenty-nine years on *A Cycle of the West*.

IV *A Defense of Poetry*

Neihardt also saw himself as an awakener, as a reteller of forgotten truths. It was in this role that he addressed the Nebraska Legislature, which had honored him with the title of Poet Laureate. One can imagine him standing on the rostrum before a group of lawyers, ranchers, and businessmen, a far tougher audience to convince than the young scholars Emerson faced at Harvard in 1837. Neihardt's laureate speech, given June 18, 1921, is his "American Scholar Address" and his defense of poetry in a practical age.

The graduate of Nebraska Normal begins his speech by discussing the relationship of poetry to education. If his listeners had not read much poetry, at least education was familiar to them. Education, Neihardt asserts, is not a mechanical process but a spiritual one, although it is practical as well. Perhaps the people's representatives perked up at the mention of "Practical education," which legislators still speak of these days. After thus getting their attention, Neihardt uses a deft transition: he says that Americans usually think of "practical" as a synonym for "profitable," but if that were true, man would be only a machine. "In its proper function, it [education] is concerned less with the problem of acquiring the means of life than with the far more difficult one of knowing what to do with life after one is in possession of the means to live."[32]

To Neihardt, the proper kind of education makes the "distinction between what man truly is and what he has": "And in this sense it is the prime function of education to make men social beings; to make them, insofar as it may be possible, citizens of all times and of all countries; to give them the widest possible comprehension of a man's relation to other men and to his physical environment; to institute sympathy for prejudice in the list of human motives. In other words, the consciousness of a individual must be extended to include race consciousness. It must be made possible for the one to live vicariously the life of the many from the beginning."

This objective of extending an individual's consciousness is also the true function of poetry, for poetic language conveys more than its literal meaning. It goes beyond man's superficial awareness, and it enables him to understand the deeper mysteries: "Something is present in the greater moments of human utterance that quite eludes your finest mesh of case, number, tense, mode. At such moments you become aware that it is a mere skeleton you have been analyzing and that some spirit lives among those dry bones." Just as man has both higher and lower functions, so does language. Moreover, Neihardt is not contemptuous of the physical life; he even endorses physical education in this speech. He simply makes the same division between Nature and the Soul that Emerson makes.[33]

Poetry is the highest form of art because it penetrates to those deepest levels of man's intellect. Music has only one dimension; painting, two; sculpture, three; but poetry adds the fourth dimension — time. It provides a means for achieving timelessness, "a means whereby men may share with each other the ancient but never old news of an immaterial world that interpenetrates and glorifies the world of sense." Poetry is a way of revelation that operates by means of symbol, rhythm, and appeal to memory. Neihardt explains these poetic devices to an audience that doubtless included many cattlemen and farmers who did not know a caesura from a cinch-strap, and he does so brilliantly. His definition of the literary symbol, for instance, is perhaps one of the best ever composed. Each symbol, Neihardt says, "is like a little door opened suddenly upon long vistas of life; and he who looks through them shall be glorified by the consciousness of his close kinship with all men in all time." Rhythm, Neihardt points out, provides a symmetry or roundness since nothing in nature is square. Rhythm is not artificial. "It is not less than the artistic manifestation of power's tendency to return upon itself, to make cycles." With Emerson, Neihardt knows that "it is not meters, but a meter-making argument that makes a poem." [34]

To Neihardt experiment in the arts is a good thing since experimentation helps keep them fresh and vital, but experiment solely for its own sake is usually bad. Many experiments in modern art reflect only the problems of modern society: "Some six or seven years ago, an exhibition of Cubist and Futurist paintings was held in various large cities of the country. Many of us went to satisfy our curiosity and some of us remained to laugh. But it was no laughing matter; for out of these grotesque daubs already leered the hideous spirit of disorganization that was then driving us on to an unthinkable catastrophe."[35] That Neihardt could not also see the humane value of words by Georges Braque, Pablo Picasso, Marcel Duchamp, Henri Matisse, Constantin Brancusi, and others displayed at the Armory Show of 1913 is a mark against him. But his blindness to their humanism is a reflection of his strong concern for the ethical value of art and for the importance of art as a teacher. He is certainly right, however, in seeing that the paintings were a response to the coming of World War I; but he did not see that some of the artists were as concerned with the need for moral values as he was.

Concerning needless and formless experimentation in poetry, Neihardt is much more acute. He could tell a genuine poet from a pretender; and he knew the difference between a useful, expressive symbolism and the excessive use of private, needlessly vague imagery. Here again his concern is that the artist should always be a moral, intellectual, and spiritual leader. His view is the Romantic ideal of Percy Bysshe Shelley: a poet is the "unacknowledged legislator of mankind," and he wants to turn the rascals out. As Neihardt bluntly explained, "It has been the claim of these misguided enthusiasts and poseurs that they are writing democratic verse; whereas, their product is so exclusively aristocratic, as someone has aptly remarked, that in the majority of cases no one but the authors can tell with any degree of certainty just what it is the authors are trying to communicate."[36]

Neihardt's poetic conservatism is not just Midwestern parochialism or a narrow distrust of anything new. Instead, it results from his high standards of artistic integrity. He knows that his countrymen are quick to embrace the new and to discard the old without any regard for what they may lose in the process. He is an old-fashioned Humanist (he disliked the narrow, politically conservative New Humanism of Irving Babbitt) who believed with Matthew Arnold that the critic's duty was "a disinterested endeavor to learn and propagate the best that is known and thought in the world."[37] Neihardt even studied Greek so that he could read Homer and Aeschylus in the original. Like Thoreau, he is disgusted by the reading habits of most people who read only what is easy and popular. These people deprive themselves not only of their own cultural heritage but also of a source of inspiration.

Neihardt continued his defense of poetry at greater length in *Poetic Values: Their Reality and Our Need of Them*, a series of lectures published in 1925. At the beginning of his book, he acknowledges that his are not original ideas but ones which need to be restated for every generation; and he carefully credits his sources, which range from the *Upanishads* to modern psychology textbooks. Like a good American, however, he begins with common sense, just as he began his laureate address. Like the good teacher he was, he begins with the simple and works toward the complex, trying to carry his pupils along with him. He starts by quoting the old saw, "Well, there's more truth than poetry in that," a saying which has a deeper significance.

Most people, Neihardt claims, make the mistake of separating truth from poetry when, in fact, poetry contains the most important truths. After this assertion comes a definition of poetry, which is not "hokum" set to rhyme and distributed by "Guest, Braly, and Co." but something much better. Good poetry expresses greater truths than the simple utilitarian philosophy by which most people live. Poetry is all that keeps one from converting truths into platitudes:

I know that there has been a saying to the effect that Americans worship the dollar; and it may be that the first man who said it intended to make a literal statement of an observed fact. But the saying has passed so often through the bath of the multitude that its meaning has been washed away, and it has become, as so many tremendous statements of truth have become by the same process, no more than a harmless platitude — harmless, indeed, as the most explosive utterance of the Nazarene have become harmless — so harmless that even a hypocrite may juggle them freely, and they won't go off![38]

Besides providing relief from platitudes, poetry is also the only way men have of linking the objective with the subjective, the real with the imaginary. Neihardt asserts that neither the Western, utilitarian, materialistic view of life nor the otherworldly Eastern philosophy is entirely correct. Poetry is what bridges the gap between and gives a balanced philosophy to live by. No one individual possesses the whole truth. Therefore, Neihardt argues, "We shall have to make out with a conception of relative truth whereby we can live; but this must be the broadest humanly realizable truth; and that is what the common-sense man certainly has not. . . ."

The artist can provide his audience with a broad, humane conception of truth, expressed in the form of an art object. Poets, painters, and musicians are alike in that they all have visions of the truth. What makes art different from other forms of communication is that the artist's truth cannot be stated or paraphrased directly; "a sense of it must somehow be induced." The best poetry accomplishes this induction by using symbols which never seem to lose their meaning. Thus good poetry provides a permanent source of both joy and wisdom: "It is because human life is vexed with ceaseless change that the relative stabilities of art are precious to us; and those relative stabilities are not illusory, for even in change there are principles that endure, and there is an essential humanness that, at least for our brief planetary life, is constant. We cannot live humanly without an abiding sense of such constancies; and it is by virtue of what we have called the creative dream that these may be vividly realized." This same permanence Neihardt sought to achieve in his own poetry. He tried to discover and express fundamental principles common to all men in all times. That he often succeeded is a measure of his value to the future.

CHAPTER 2

Lyric Years

THE best way to read John Neihardt's lyric poetry is to follow
the advice he gives in the preface to his *Lyric and Dramatic
Poems* (1965). Neihardt writes that the collected lyrics constitute
"what may be called a spiritually progressive sequence, beginning
with the experience of groping youth and rising to the self-
fulfillment of parenthood."[1] This sequence was not at first
deliberately planned; it occurred because Neihardt's lyric poetry is
intensely personal and reflects the progression of his own life. By
following this sequence, the reader can see two kinds of development, the personal and the poetic. In the concluding lyrics, the personal references disappear as the poet achieves what he termed "the
loss of the sense of self in cosmic awareness."[2]

I A Bundle of Myrrh

The first group of lyrics in *Lyric and Dramatic Poems* comes from
Neihardt's second published volume of poetry, *A Bundle of Myrrh*.
After the failure of his juvenile epic, *The Divine Enchantment*
(published when he was nineteen but written three years earlier),
Neihardt turned to shorter forms with much greater success. *A Bundle of Myrrh* is a collection of lyrics, most of which deal with love,
both fulfilled and unfulfilled. They are very much a young man's
poems, full of emotional assertions. After circulation in manuscript
for some time, these lyrics were published by the Outing Company
in 1907 and met with almost universal critical approval. Even con-
sidering that the years just before the founding of *Poetry* did not see
much good, new American poetry and that poetry with any degree
of originality whatsoever was likely to be well received, the praise
heaped on a little book by an almost unknown young man from
Nebraska is surprising. The New York *Times*, which contained the
most enthusiastic review, asserted that "the book is not just a collec-

tion of short poems but a symphony with the first keynote the riotous joy of the flesh, working up in the last songs to the voice of penitence, the birth of the spirit and of vision."[3] Another reviewer, however, was somewhat worried about the excess of passion in some poems and expressed the hope that "he will not make the mistake of thinking that nudity is strength, and that in order to show that one is independent and virile he must exhibit all his emotions unclothed rather than clothed by the imagination."[4] Throughout Neihardt's early career, genteel reviewers thought him too bold and too brutal; yet such a criticism seems ludicrous in retrospect since Neihardt is the most moral of poets. Still, the passion in these early lyrics attracted Mona Martinsen and persuaded her to leave Paris for Omaha to marry the poet.

A Bundle of Myrrh does not deserve the high praise it received, but its first reviewers were not entirely wrong. Although most of the poems are apprentice work, some do show indications of Neihardt's future power; and they are charged with his characteristic energy and exuberance — even with too much energy and exuberance in some cases. Emotion is often stated directly instead of being dramatized, and the poet's attitude is like Shelley's in the famous line from "Ode to the West Wind," "I fall upon the thorns of life! I bleed!" Neihardt's volume contains a bloody bundle of poems that pant and sigh, ache and yearn, grope and dream, whistle and wail. It is a collection of ecstatic visions in which the poet becomes, in the words of one poem, a "chaser of dim vast figures." Above all, these poems are Romantic in every sense of the word. Shelley's "West Wind" blows through them like a prairie tornado, and the poet is a twentieth-century Alastor or Endymion searching for an ideal love. All atune to the "currents of the Universal Being" circulating through him, he gets impulses from the vernal wood; and, like Whitman, he finds letters from God dropped in the street every day. Like Tennyson's knights, whom Neihardt so admired, he searches for some vague, poetic grail.

A Bundle of Myrrh begins with "Lines in Late March," a perfect example of the William Cullen Bryant syndrome. Instead of letting spring be its own excuse for existence, Neihardt moralizes the life out of it. Like Browning's Pippa, the poet is happy, happy, and all his doubts vanish. "I want to believe the songs I hear from the fenceposts!" he cries, and the reader hopes that these fenceposts have singing birds on them.[5] In spite of such embarrassingly bad lines as "Have the green grass and blue sky testified falsely?", the poem does contain one good image: new grass is "the green that winds up the slough." This image appears in several other poems as a fresh, specific way of showing the progress of spring.

In "The Witless Musician," the next poem in the volume, the poet's lover is imagined as a violin on which he plays a metaphor which Neihardt also uses in an early short story, "Vylin." As he does in all these early poems, Neihardt sees physical love as a great, dark mystery, almost as D. H. Lawrence does; but, at this point in his career, Neihardt lacked Lawrence's ability to dramatize that mystery. When the poet touches his "Violin," he says, "I lay my hands upon her with that divine thrill in my fingertips,/ . . . Which a harpist feels when he reaches for a ravishing chord." But the male does not simply manipulate the female; she also takes part in the "harmony" of the concert.

"The Sound My Spirit Calls You" continues this theme; and although the imagery seems somewhat hackneyed nowadays, it does indicate Neihardt's experiments with ways to visualize sound and to hear pictures. "Soft as the kiss of the Stream to the drooping Leaf" is an example. Like all of the poems in *A Bundle of Myrrh*, it shows considerable mastery of the technical elements of poetry, of what Neihardt later termed the "conscious manipulation of sound." It is written in free verse, like several other poems in this collection, but Neihardt later abandoned this technique. Here he is still trying out his skills, investigating what to keep and what to discard.

"At Parting" is a quiet, simple poem that avoids the emotionalism of some other poems, but it is still a bit too vague and dreamy to be completely successful. Like most Romantic poets, Neihardt is at his best when he can find a concrete object or event in which to embody and give life to his vision, to tie it down to earth so that it cannot soar off into infinity, leaving his readers behind. In this poem, he tries to capture

> That ever luring and elusive thing —
> A song that I conceived, but could not sing;
> A dream I dreamed but, waking, could not live;
> Sweet wine for which my goblet was a sieve!

"Longing," the next poem, is perhaps the worst poem in *A Bundle of Myrrh* because it sees as good a point of view which Neihardt usually condemns, as well he should condemn it. One may pardon the overexuberance, the excessive lushness of other poems in this volume — in fact, one may enjoy their youthful vigor and vitality;

but it is difficult to be at all sympathetic toward "Longing." In this poem, the speaker wants only to escape to some perfect hideaway:

> There in the wilds with only you to love me
> And none to hate,
> I could feel Something good and strong above me,
> More kind than Fate.

This going into nature is not to "front only the essential facts of life," as Thoreau did at Walden, nor is it going to nature for inspiration or understanding; it is merely a simpleminded desire to avoid problems:

> I could forget the aches of hope and failing,
> That with slow fires consume
> This futile flesh that goes on groping, wailing
> Toward the gloom.

Anytime a robust young man talks about "futile flesh" and consuming fires, the result has to be phony. Fortunately for posterity, Neihardt seldom indulged in this kind of self-pity. In all his best works, the theme is struggle; and life has value because men are willing to struggle for it. Neihardt takes the bromidic motto of Tennyson's "Ulysses," "to strive, to seek, to find, and not to yield," and he transforms it into a profound appreciation of what life can be for those who refuse to surrender but who dedicate their lives to achieving a real dream, not a quixotic "Impossible Dream" but a real vision of the good life.

"Should We Forget," the next poem in the sequence, is a harmless sentimental trifle as is its successor, "Come Back." For "In Autumn," Neihardt uses the same verse form as "Longing" to express the poet's refusal to succumb to a gray, autumnal mood because his lover has brightened the gloom. All these ideas are standard poetic stock, but Neihardt tries in the next series of poems to get closer to the visionary gleam. Always interested in what he calls "spiritual things," he wants to find ways of expressing states of mind. Two of these poems, "The Subtle Spirit" and "The Temple of the Great Outdoors," are, like Neihardt's first epic, *The Divine Enchantment*, too misty to have much meaning. "Chaser of Dim Vast Figures," however, works a refreshing change on the Romantic quest for a vision of ideal beauty. The Chaser, which Neihardt clearly identifies with himself, surrenders his futile pursuit when he meets a real woman:

> And in my hair I felt your fingers move,
> And felt your woman's lips about my face,
> And felt your cool cheek on my burning cheek.
> So I have lost the wish to dream again.

This poem demonstrates Neihardt's healthy ability to see his visionary quest, his dream of love and glory, with some detachment; and the poem is perhaps the most successful in *A Bundle of Myrrh*.

"There Was a Voice" is similar in theme, but it has a different verse form: it is a sort of chant or incantation in free verse. The beginning is unpromising, with vague feelings of sympathy with nature and the "Tender, formless, vast unworshipped God," but the vague forms suddenly become visible, the mysteries are embodied in a real woman, and the poem comes to life. Neihardt continues his experimentation with different verse forms and different types of poems in "Retrospect," an attempt at a seduction poem modeled after Christopher Marlowe's "The Passionate Shepherd to His Love" and Andrew Marvell's "To His Coy Mistress." Its successor, "Recognition," is also an attempt by Neihardt to assert his identity with the great poets of antiquity, something which he tried to do throughout his career. In *Poetic Values*, he stresses the poet's link with the past and his responsibility to that past; but in "Recognition" the past is trivialized.

> O let us journey back to Thessaly,
> And from these echoes build the olden song!
> Hast thou forgotten, through these ages long,
> The tinkle of the sheep-bells and the shrill
> Glad oaten reeds of shepherds on the hill?

In a recent television interview, Neihardt spoke of the frank sensuality of these poems. Though they seem rather pale today, one can imagine that a reader of 1907 might think them quite bold. "If This Be Sin," for instance, begins,

> Can this be sin?
> This ecstasy of arms and eyes and lips,
> This thrilling of caressing finger-tips,
> This toying with incomparable hair?
> (I close my dazzled eyes, you are so fair!)
> This answer of caress to fond caress,
> This exquisite maternal tenderness?

> How could so much beauty enter in,
> If this be sin?

Apparently the future Mrs. Neihardt had a strong taste for sentimentality; otherwise, she would not have been won by such poetry. In "Let Down Your Hair," which is even worse, the poor poet is in thrall to his love and cries out, "I faint before the dazzle of your breast." He pants, "I am athirst — your tresses fall like rain." Even day and night are personified as women waiting for the poet's passionate embrace. He wants Night, a "Titan-Woman," to share his bed; and she comes willingly with the moon upon her forehead and the stars twinkling in her hair. "The Morning Girl" is no less ardent:

> Then her pure and dazzling breast
> Made with joy my senses swoon,
> As she burned from crest to crest
> Upward to the noon.

Like the speaker in Edna St. Vincent Millay's famous poem, "First Fig," the poet-lover wants to live a short but incandescent life. In "Let Me Live Out My Years," he prays, "Let me go quickly like a candle light/Snuffed out just at the heyday of the glow!"

The climax to this voluptuous indulgence comes near the end of *A Bundle of Myrrh* in a poem that tries to explain the poet's desperate hunger for love, beauty, experience, and excitement. "Prayer of an Alien Soul" contains three consecutive "Ah me's" and other excesses, but the reader who knows Neihardt's later career can forgive them since he can sympathize with the poet's desire to fulfill the destiny he first glimpsed as a boy. The word "alien" appears elsewhere in Neihardt's work to mean the one who stands outside, who cannot yet capture his vision in poetry. His reach exceeds his grasp, and this fact frustrates him. The young poet is not yet a bard, not yet a member of the classic company, not yet immortal. This yearning for immortality may seem the height of vanity; but, as Neihardt explained it, it was a defense mechanism, a way of keeping faith with the better work ahead of him. These early poems were javelins "hurled at momentary doubt." As Neihardt concludes his prayer,

> I hear the far cry of my destiny
> Whose meaning sings beyond the furthest sun.

> I faint in these red chains, and I would 'rise and run.
> O Center of the Scheme,
> Star-Flinger, Beauty-Builder, Shaping Dream.

Though the poems in *A Bundle of Myrrh* are of varying quality, most of them show the same drive. Their intense energy, which occasionally overflows into sentimentality or even bathos, was a healthy sign of better work to come when Neihardt's poetic dynamo was properly charged.

II   *"A Vision of Woman"*

The second group of lyrics in the *Lyric and Dramatic Poems* is entitled "A Vision of Woman." These five longer poems were published in *Man-Song* (1909), Neihardt's second collection, which received even more critical praise than his first. Bliss Carman, who was at that time a highly respected poet, wrote in the New York *Times* that Neihardt's work contained "The lyric intensity of a naive and passionate voice"; and he praised Neihardt's many wholesome qualities.[6] Though Carman welcomed Neihardt as a fresh, vigorous, new voice, he worried a little about a certain "brutality of expression," thus betraying his own gentility. Another reviewer was even more enthusiastic: "Here is poetry, virile, full of red blood, man's blood, quivering with his passion, singing in his triumph quite untrammeled by convention of thought or usage. The sweep of it carries the reader with it, the elemental male is singing of life and achievement, giving glorious tribute to love and to generation."[7]

"A Vision of Woman," the first of these five poems, is a long meditation in blank verse that is less emotional, less consciously "poetic," and more conversational than the poems of *A Bundle of Myrrh*. It seems as if the young man's ardor has cooled somewhat; he is still a lover but is more philosophical, less blinded by the light from dazzling breasts, and more intent on finding universal significance in his particular love. He begins by denying the beast in himself and asserts that he has been calmed by "a sense of the enduring things." His calm, however, is only temporary as he remembers their first meeting:

> The smoldering ashes of old primal lusts
> The strident fiddles wakened and the wine.
> And so I bought you — paid the stated price —
> Washed out my scruples in a flood of wine.

Here, as elsewhere in his early poetry, Neihardt sounds like the English Decadents. In this passage, one hears particular echoes of Ernest Dowson's "Non Sum Qualis Eram Bonae sub Regno Cynarae."

Love conquers lust, however, as the power of Neihardt's woman transforms this tawdry affair into a poetic vision; hence the poem's title.

> I touched you — and 'twas Helen that I touched;
> And in my blood young Paris lived again;
> And all the grief and gloom of Illium,
> . . . .
> Seemed naught for one round burning kiss from you!

William Carlos Williams said it better in "Asphodel, That Greeny Flower," one of the greatest of modern love poems.

> All women are not Helen
> I know that,
> but have Helen in their hearts.

The poet-lover Neihardt next embarks upon a meditation which might be subtitled "The Female in History," and he does pretty well with it:

> Once more for me the Carthaginian pyre
> Built day by day amid the dusk of sordid things;
> And that sad Queen whom all the world shall love
> Because one man forsook her far away
> Followed with tearless tragic eyes the sail
> That bellied skyward in a wind of Fate.
> And through the night the wail of Hecuba
> Brought back the Thracian sorrow, made it mine:
> While in the aching hush that followed it
> Red drop by drop I heard the Virgin's blood.

In these lines, the blank verse is calm, sure, and stately. The imagery is specific and striking, and the remembrances engage one's genuine sympathy. Neihardt is now beginning to deal with tragedy instead of pathos. Yet the entire poem is not on the same level as these lines, for the poet is still developing both his craft and his philosophy of life.

"Woman-Wine," the next poem in this sequence, expresses the

same theme in a different form. Instead of slow, stately blank verse,
it is a lilting song reminiscent of Byron's "Maid of Athens." Again,
the poet is transported by his discovery of the eternal female, by his
drinking from the cup of woman-wine:

> Awful burning lips of Thais,
> Kiss me back Persepolis!
> Break my heart — I'm Menelaus!
> Make me Paris with a kiss!

As in the previous poem, the poet worships woman as mother, sister,
and wife. She is the possessor of a powerful Life Force which is
greater than anything man has to counter it. But, by uniting with a
woman, man gains a taste of her metaphorical magic potion:

> *Cup of sweet felicity,*
> *Cup of ancient woman-*
> *wine!*
> *Vanquished is my victory —*
> *It is mine!*

The Life Force is personified as "Eros" in the next lyric of "A Vision
of Woman" and is also identified with an Earth Mother in "Gaea,
Mother Gaea." Gaea, the ancient Titan, provides consolation when
the poet (Neihardt in one of his self-pitying moods again) comes to
her suffering from *Weltschmerz*, a common disease of young
Romantic poets. To ease his pain, he implores her to lend him some
of her natural strength; for, when he obtains this power, he will be
able to conquer his own doubts and continue his career.

"A Vision of Woman" concludes with a pleasant "Nuptial Song,"
in which "Woman" is finally united with the lover who has been
searching for her. Together, they create a proper, natural harmony
that is the best of all possible music:

> Sweeter than all other
> Songs of lip or lyre —
> Every Maid a Mother,
> Every Man a Sire;
> Joy beneath the pain warm,
> God amidst the plan,
> Field unto the Rainstorm,
> Maid unto the Man!

III   The Stranger at the Gate

The logical and biological result of marriage is "The mystery of birth," which Neihardt celebrates in *The Stranger at the Gate*, a collection published in 1912, which received still more praise from the reviewers. The genteel critics were particularly pleased because "Mr. Neihardt softens his rugged verses of revolt into a series of beautiful lyrics that hymn the mystery of new life, and give tender welcome to the stranger at the gate."[8] One would like to say that this sequence of lyrics marks yet another stage in Neihardt's steady poetic development and that it points forward toward even better work to come; unfortunately, such is not the case. Like most men, Neihardt went gaga at the thought of fatherhood; for he had just had his first child to whom he dedicated *The Stranger at the Gate*. The fine, hard edge of his poetic sword, which he had been honing into an Excalibur, went dull as a butter knife. Instead of investigating the mystery of birth and trying to discover its significance, instead of recapturing its joy in clear, sharp, vivid images, Neihardt retreats into trivialities. One wonders how an intelligent, sensitive poet, a man who loved truth and honored purity of line, a man who liked to work with his hands and lived a vigorous outdoor life, could write such awful silly, insipid poetry as this:

> Mark the downy flower-coats
> In the hollyhocks!
> Hark the cooing Wheat-Soul
> Weaving for her flocks!
> Croon-time, June-time,
> Moon of baby frocks.

Other poems in this collection are filled with such phrases as "dappled gloaming," "A little Stranger," and "Blessed Comer."

In almost all his work, Neihardt maintains a profound religious spirit which partakes of the best of all faiths and all scriptures from the *Upanishads* to the oral stories of American Indian medicine men. Here, in "The Child's Heritage," he resorts to the least profound elements of Christianity, a Sunday-school sentimentality:

> A tattered cloak may be thy dole
> And thine the roof that Jesus had:
> The broidered garment of the soul
> Shall keep thee purple-clad!

Only on a few occasions does the real poet lift aside this ruffled curtain to see clearly and freshly; one such example comes at the conclusion of "Break of Day" with this vivid simile:

> Glowing through the gray rack
> Breaks the Day —
> Like a burning haystack
> Twenty farms away!

IV   The "Poet's Town"

Of all the lyrics in *Lyric and Dramatic Poems*, those most likely to endure are grouped under the heading "A Poet's Town." Written between 1908 and 1912, they did not appear as a separate collection. These poems are much less personal than the others and deal with the poet's relationship to his society. The poet's own emotional problems are unimportant except as they affect how he sees the people and institutions around him. For this reason, these poems constitute the final stage in Neihardt's development from a love-lorn youth to a proud parent to a responsible citizen of the world. More conventional in form and style than some of the early lyrics (because by this time Neihardt had pretty much abandoned the various free-verse forms), they also avoid the trite and sentimental. This restraint is probably a result of Neihardt's turning away from intense personal experiences toward sympathy for the experiences of others on his way to achieving what he called "cosmic awareness."

"The Poet's Town," which begins this series of poems, is about a happy place for a young dreamer to grow up. Surrounded by pastoral beauty, the "outseeking bard," as Walt Whitman would call him, learns to see with "mystic eyes" which make even an ordinary country town seem extraordinary. Young Neihardt, growing up in Nebraska, must have dreamed the same dreams as young Vachel Lindsay in Springfield, Illinois; for "The Poet's Town" shares its central theme with Lindsay's "Springfield Magical." In both poems, the supposedly philistine Midwest provides a good place for the young poet to mature despite his townspeople's distrust of art.

For both Lindsay and Neihardt, the struggle is between the heroic ideals which the fledgling poet gets from books and the profit ethic of his elders who neither understand nor value his vision. As Neihardt put it,

> Corn for buyers and cattle —
> But what could the dreamer sell?
> Echoes of cloudy battle?
> Music from Heaven and hell?

Neihardt's battle against these buyers is a common theme in his work. He often finds new ways to say "Greed is the root of evil," and he flails the selfish rich. Although he willingly accepted the necessary genteel poverty of his profession, Neihardt resented the same men that Vachel Lindsay excoriated in "Bryan, Bryan, Bryan, Bryan" — the plutocrats, "With dollar signs upon their coats." In a cancelled preface for *The Song of Hugh Glass*, Neihardt wrote bitterly that "praise of Helen paid no grocer bills!" In spite of such hostility, the would-be poet dreams while working in the fields to feed his body while his mind is fed on Greece and Rome.

In "The Poet's Advice," Neihardt warns of the price one must pay for choosing art over business. Since "the world loves not its dreamers overmuch," to be different requires strength of character and a belief in one's own ultimate destiny. Without these, one is doomed to a life of shallow conformity; and Neihardt is always concerned with the levelling tendency of modern democracy. Other poets, Pound and Eliot for example, simply rejected democracy and went to Europe to live under more aristocratic forms of government; but Neihardt was too much a patriot to do so. He disliked, sometimes to the point of contempt, the mass of men, for as he wrote in the cancelled preface,

> O Demos, you have spoken — be it so!
> World-wide ascends the paen to the crowd,
> For you are very big and very loud
> And sacrosanct in being loud and big!
> You wear the crown and the judicial wig;
> Vox populi, vox dei — we must hear:
> A million dunces, melted mould a seer,
> A hundred million mortals make a god!

But, instead of leaving for Paris, Neihardt stayed and, like the good schoolteacher he was, tried to educate the dunces with such books as *Poetic Values*, with his readings and lecture tours, and with his book reviews. Vachel Lindsay wore himself out trying to preach a similar "Gospel of Beauty" and ended his own life; but Little Bull Buffalo had more faith and more staying power and this enabled him to stand alone and live. He knew his own imperfections, but he persevered, as he advised others to do:

> Your rhymes? — Some nimbler footed have been worse.
> What broken trumpet echoes from the van
> Where march the cohorts of Immortal Verse!
> Well — one must be a poet if one can.

Following the first two lyrics of "A Poet's Town," which establish its main theme, is a group of nature poems in which the poet discovers Nature's great organic power. The poet's mission is to testify to that power, just as one might testify to a belief in the divinity of Jesus. In "April Theology," Spring awakens the poet's sense of identity with natural processes, which are as holy to him as any scripture. Instead of kneeling humbly in prayer to some anthropomorphic deity, he sees the deity in himself because he too is a part of the life process. Like Emerson in the joyous introduction to *Nature*, Neihardt becomes "part or parcel of God." Some lines of this poem sound very much like Whitman's expression of a similar theme in "Song of Myself." Neihardt writes,

> This something called self is a part, but the world
>   is the whole of me.
> I am one with these growers, these singers, these
>   earnest becomers —
> Co-heirs of the summer to be and the past aeons of summers!

By seeing nature clearly and fully, he becomes "close-knit in the fabric of things." In "April Theology," Neihardt expresses a mature, intelligent, life-enhancing philosophy. If a poet is to continue after he has spent his first burst of lyric energy, he must have a philosophy, something to "prop" his mind. His "prop" may be a conventional religion like Eliot's Anglo-Catholicism, a spiritualist "Vision" like Yeats's, an aesthetic idealism like Wallace Stevens', or simply a dogged determination to come through somehow. What sustained Neihardt was his belief in the spiritual power of the natural world, a belief he shared with his Indian friends.

Such a belief enables the poet to look at the world with a sense of wonder, which Neihardt expresses in these poems. "On First Seeing the Ocean" speaks of a "dreamed of wonder," but the poet is surprised to discover that the ocean holds no new glory for him: he has already experienced the same sense of infinite space on the rolling prairies of his native state. To Whitman, the ocean was a mother rocking the cradle of life; to Neihardt, the prairie mother, the Maka of the Sioux, swelled with a similar rhythm. The prairie storms that Neihardt portrays so brilliantly in his later work also appear in these lyrics as metaphors for the storm of life. Before such storms comes a dreadful calm, the wind freshens, and the rain drives down — refreshing, life-giving, but also fierce and savage.

In many works by Neihardt, the storms and struggles of living are depicted as good things. In "Prayer for Pain," the poet prays for the pain of struggle because struggle *is* life, and life without struggle or pain is too bland, too dull, too empty. "Battle-Cry" also is a prayer, this time one asking for the will to fight. This will to fight is what defines the poet as a person, and it is what makes him a man. Only a coward refuses to face his destiny. Like Tennyson's Ulysses and the speaker of William Ernest Henley's "Invictus," Neihardt believes that every individual must master his fate. If he does not fight for such mastery, he dooms himself to be a mere servant of chance. This belief also is the frontier ethic, the famous code of the West, so often debased in popular versions. Although Neihardt was born too late to wear a Colt on his hip, he engaged in literary shootouts against both the effete genteel tradition and the exclusive lost generation; and, in his poem "The Lyric," poetry is seen as a weapon in such battles: "Hurl the lyric swift and true/Like a shaft of Doom!" The poet flings his "mighty song" against an invisible enemy; and, though his enemy may be invisible, his battle is certainly real enough; for no quixotic tilting at windmills exists for Neihardt.

The invisible enemy is identified in the next major group of poems in "A Poet's Town," which deals with economics, politics, and war; but, in all of them, the poet's adversary is greed. In "Money," the poet stops to ask a man why he digs his life away beside the road. When the man replies that he is digging for wealth, the poet lectures him on the futility of his life and tells him, "you are the vassal of a thing you make!" Of course, no one is for greed, but Neihardt does more than just preach; he tried, throughout his entire career, to demonstrate — in lectures, poems, articles, reviews, novels, short stories, and plays — that the constant search for financial gain is self-defeating, futile, and degrading. This theme is common enough in literature, but Neihardt develops it more than any other modern American writer, with the possible exception of John Steinbeck, because he saw the business ethic as endangering everything in which he believed. In *Poetic Values* and in his laureate address, he speaks often of the need to change the American system of values.

Though he seldom worshiped by an established creed, Neihardt is a deeply religious man who believes that one must drive the money changers from the temple of art and that one should spend one's time on more important things. These "spiritual things" are not just abstract ideals or vague dreams; to Neihardt, they are real as dollar bills and far more permanent.

"Song of the Turbine Wheel" develops this idea further and makes a good companion poem to Vachel Lindsay's "Factory Windows Are Always Broken" since both poets wonder about the human cost of a machine civilization. As heirs of Romanticism, they resent the encroachment of industrialism upon the natural world; and both have something of the Luddite who wishes to destroy machines in them. As Midwesterners, they celebrate the village and the prairie; and they distrust the city though they may find it exciting for a little while. Though they were not opposed to all development, they worried about the loss of a value system in which they earnestly believed. Neihardt's turbine wheel, for example, brags and blusters about his ability to groan on through day and night; but the rollicking brook laughs at him. The turbine is chained; but the brook is free and easy, a fishing stream on warm June days. By the end of the poem, the turbine begins to sympathize with the rippling waters:

> And, bound as I am where the darkness lingers,
> I half forgive their careless way,
> Such soothing, tinkling tunes they play —
> All with their icy fingers.

This intrusion of a cold, gray, ugly, impersonal, and often destructive machine into the American garden has been a basic theme in its literature for a hundred years.[9] It is closely related to the literary convention of the pastoral which dates from ancient Greece. But for Neihardt the intrusion into pastoral nature by the machine represents more than simply the violation of a literary convention. When Thoreau at Walden Pond sees and hears the locomotive, it only distracts and annoys him, but he also resents the railroad's exploitation of cheap Irish labor. When the railroad bisects Sioux Territory in Neihardt's epic poems or in his *Black Elk Speaks*, however, it is a much more serious matter — it is not a nuisance but a tragedy. The railroad carries miners and settlers which require troops to protect them; it brings buffalo hunters to slaughter the source of food, clothing, and fuel; it destroys a culture; it replaces

spiritual values with material ones; it signifies a victory of flesh over
spirit, of money over honor.

For these reasons, Neihardt wages a lonely fight against progress
as it is usually defined. Henry Adams, in a famous chapter of his
autobiography, compares thirteenth-century unity, as symbolized by
the Virgin of Chartres Cathedral, to twentieth-century diversity, as
symbolized by the great dynamo he saw at the Great Exposition of
1900. Neihardt found his own symbol of unity in the great hoop of
the Sioux nation. Though the hoop had already been broken by his
time, Neihardt tried to keep its memory intact.

"The Red Wind Comes" and its companion piece, "A Cry of the
People," concern one possible reaction against the triumph of Mam-
mon. Though Neihardt carefully indicates that both poems were
written years before the Russian Revolution and cannot be taken as a
partisan political stance, he does regard the poems as prophetic.
"Surely," he wrote in a preface to the collected lyrics, "the 'Red
Wind' is blowing out of the East across the world. Surely the 'Cry of
the People' is heard more and more around our troubled planet."
These two poems are "a young poet's response to the social injustices
of his time, when a good man would work a hard ten-hour day for a
dollar or less, if he could only find work to do." Neihardt knew such
poverty since he had worked as a potato-picker for the lowest of
wages, and he also knew how grinding poverty could crush man's
spirit and darken his hopes for a better life. Even recently he expressed his sympathy with those young people who, with Bob Dylan,
hear the winds of change still blowing.[10]

Neihardt begins "The Red Wind Comes" with a discussion of the
"July bombast" that Americans praise so highly. The liberties once
fought for are useless, he asserts, unless Americans give more than
lip service to them. The battle to realize these ideals that is coming
will be against the System, now controlled by plutocrats whose time
has past: "Behold the signs prophetic of thy fall,/ O Dynast of the
Fat!" Here Neihardt "beats out the rhythms of his age," to use Paul
Rosenfeld's criterion for the good poet; for his reformist spirit is akin
to that of the muckrakers. Because Neihardt has no specific target for
his wrath, his lack of specificity weakens the poem somewhat; but it
still has force today, especially in its last lines:

> Beware the Furies stirring in the gloom!
> They mutter from the mines, the mills, the slums!
> No lie shall stay or mitigate thy doom —
> *The Red Wind Comes!*

"Cry of the People" is equally passionate in its assault on the status quo. The "workers and makers," Neihardt says, will march on the owners, using "The world's heart-beat for a drum." Using the rhetoric of the *Communist Manifesto*, Neihardt writes of workers "snapping the chains of ages." The dark night of injustice and servitude has ended, and the oppressed people are "marching into the day!" But Neihardt is intelligent enough to realize that the System will not yield easily to the assaults of a single man, and "Czolgosz" is a good poem about this theme. Although Leon Czolgosz, an anarchist, assassinated President McKinley, the government continues unchanged. Though the American Brutus has murdered a man he thinks to be a tyrant, "Our Caesar has not flesh to feel the knife;/ Still Caesar lives — and this is not the end!" History is more powerful than individuals, and their insipid acts are usually futile. McKinley is gone, but his death has not ushered in the worker's paradise. The individual, however, must struggle on nevertheless, using whatever weapons he has. In Neihardt's case, the weapon is poetry; and "O Lyric Master!," which follows "Czolgosz," is a war hymn. The lyric master of which the poem speaks will give voice to the suffering and to the previously silent people; and he will awaken the mass of men to the poetic values about which Neihardt often lectured. This ideal poet will not be a mere music maker; he will be the visionary bard that Neihardt dreamed of becoming. The people desperately need such a poet:

> Hungry we cried to our singers — our singers have
>   flung us a crust!
> Choked with the smoke of the battle, staggering,
>   weary with blows,
> We cried for a flagon of music — they gave us the
>   dew of a rose!
> Gewgaw goblets they gave us, jewelled and crystalline,
> But filled with the tears of a weakling. Better
>   a gourd — and wine!

Neihardt's poetry actually did play a small part in the struggle against social injustice in the years immediately before World War I. Clarence Darrow once used "Battle-Cry" in his final remarks to a jury, and Samuel Gompers recited the same poem at a convention of the American Federation of Labor. The poem was also used in a speech by a famous French socialist editor.[11] "Battle-Cry" is not a particularly good poem, but one can understand how its ringing prayer for courage and strength of character might appeal to such men. One can even imagine a football coach posting a copy of these lines on the locker-room wall:

> Not for the glory of winning,
> Not for the fear of the night;
> Shunning the battle is sinning —
> O spare me the heart to fight!

This group of inspirational lyrics concludes with two poems written in 1914, the year of the apocalypse, "Katharsis" and "The Farmer's Thanksgiving." The subject of these two poems is Neihardt's attitude toward the Great War, which he believed was a result of the greed and stupidity that he had decried in the preceding poems. A "canting generation" has brought the horror of war upon itself, but it will perhaps provide a catharsis, a cleansing, so that men may once again be true to what is best in them, and "The land shall know a more dynamic life." While the "war to end wars" rages in Europe, America has found a better way to live. In contrast to "the might a Kaiser yields," the army of farmers goes forth to harvest the results of the previous spring when "golden volleys broke/ From batteries of seeders." When this army's victory is at hand, it is one for all that is healthy and humane. "The Farmer's Thanksgiving," a simple poem, ends with a fine happy, American song:

> Lo, where like stacked triumphant arms
> The corn shocks dot yon rise!
> Let golden bombs on all the farms
> Now burst in pumpkin pies!
> And let us sing, for we have won
> As never wins the sword;
> And know that our good fight is done,
> Be praises to the Lord!

In the last poems of "A Poet's Town," Neihardt returns to more personal subject matter; but the speaker of these lyrics is no longer a self-pitying youth. Instead, the poet is discovering what Neihardt called "cosmic consciousness" in which the individual fuses his soul with the transcendent All, with the Oversoul of Emerson and Whitman. Neihardt's song is not an individual complaint but is "Kin to all the songs that are." In "Outward," for example, the poet sails toward some ultimate destination just as Emily Dickinson's inland soul does in its outward journey to the sea in one of her famous poems. His final goal is the mystical union of self and soul, which leads to perfect peace; and Walt Whitman describes a similar experience in stanza 5 of "Song of Myself." This cosmic consciousness is equivalent to the Hindu Nirvana which Neihardt explained in *Poetic Values* as "not to be regarded as non-existence, but rather as universal existence."

Indeed, the order of the collected lyrics is analogous to the three stages for achieving Nirvana which he outlines in *Poetic Values:*

First: The Waking Consciousness, that in which men vividly conceive of themselves as individuals and are exclusively aware of everyday experiences. . . .
Second: The State of Dream Sleep. Says the *Upanishad:* "In the dream-state it (the individual self) moves up and down, and fashions for itself as gods many forms."
Third: The State of Deep Sleep. Therein the illusory sense of individuality is lost, with all its suffering merged in Brahman.[12]

In "When I Have Gone Weird Ways," Neihardt describes this final dissolution of self. The poem is an epitaph that is next to the last poem in "A Poet's Town," a section that marks the end of the first stage in Neihardt's poetic career. This poem is also an assertion of immortality and of the primary importance of spiritual values. The mourners should not weep for him, the poet says,

> But give my body to the funeral pyre,
> And bid the laughing fire,
> Eager and strong and swift as my desire,
> Scatter my subtle essence into Space —
> Free me of Time and Place.

In "L'Envoi," the last poem in "A Poet's Town," Neihardt ends this quest for Nirvana with this thought:

> My God and I shall interknit
> As rain and Ocean, breath and Air;
> And O, the luring thought of it
> Is prayer!

When John Neihardt ended the first phase of his career, he had published by the age of thirty-one three volumes of lyric verse which, with the exception of the lamentable poems about fatherhood, show both a steady improvement and the development of a mature personal philosophy. While these lyrics share some of the defects of American poetry common between 1900 and 1914, others are still quite readable. Romanticism had run its course through the nineteenth century; and the new spirit in poetry, signaled by the founding of the magazine *Poetry* in 1912, had not arrived. For these reasons, Neihardt lacked a vitalizing intellectual climate in which to write, as, for example, one scholar's list of poets who were active in the late nineteenth and early twentieth centuries indicates: ". . . Riley and Field, Paul Laurence Dunbar; the lady poets Edith Matilda Thomas, Louise Chandler Moulton, Elizabeth Stoddard, Louise Imogen Gurney, and Lizette Woodward Reese; the perfectionists Aldrich, Gilder, Bunner, and Sherman; Ambrose Bierce, Richard Hovey, Stephen Crane, Father Tabb, Henry Van Dyke, Madison Cawein, Lloyd Mifflin, George Santayana."[13] Others were William Vaughn Moody, Percy Mackaye, and a few even less memorable. The only major American poet to publish a collection between 1900 and 1911 was E. A. Robinson. According to Roy Harvey Pearce, who suggests some reasons for this unfortunate period, the poets of this era had no definite audience and also lacked the sense of the fresh awakening of cultural independence that had been announced by Emerson fifty years earlier. American culture was becoming more complex; and, as a result, the poet was less certain about his place in it.[14] This situation helps explain Neihardt's distrust of the machine and his constant search for a way to live the good life in a difficult time.

If one compares Neihardt's work to other poetry published during these lean years, he fares pretty well. Since his best poems are equal to the best of his era, his excellent reviews were not the result of critical stupidity. These lyric years were, however, a time of testing for him, of experimenting with techniques, and of searching for values. By his thirty-first year, he was a mature poet with a definite point of view and with a sure knowledge of his future goals. He was now ready to begin his life work, *A Cycle of the West*, which occupied him for the next thirty years. He had prepared for this herculean labor — and "herculean" is correct since Neihardt wanted to follow the Greek way of epic heroism by investigating the West in his early prose. Indeed, he used lyric poetry, prose fiction, and even poetic drama as a kind of literary apprenticeship to prepare for his major work.

CHAPTER 3

Poetic Drama and Prose Fiction

DURING Neihardt's long literary apprenticeship, he tried his
hand at all forms of literature with varying degrees of success.
Though his short stories were sought by magazine editors and
though his poetic drama "Agrippina" evinced considerable promise,
Neihardt came to believe, about 1912, that any additional time spent
on these forms was a betrayal of his true work, *A Cycle of the West;*
as a result, he almost abandoned prose fiction, poetic drama, and the
lyric. When he returned to fiction after *A Cycle* had been completed,
he produced a work of the highest quality, *When the Tree Flowered.*

I *Poetic Drama*

Like many of his contemporaries, Neihardt experimented with
poetic drama, and, like them, he failed. By the early twentieth century, social-realist drama had conquered the stage, largely by default
since no other form of drama had any vitality. The English Romantic
poets — Byron, Shelley, Keats, and Tennyson, all of whom wrote
verse plays — had tried to revive the tradition of Elizabethan drama;
but blank-verse tragedy now seemed a hopeless anachronism. In a
famous letter, Henrik Ibsen, founder of the new drama, declared the
iambic-pentameter tragedy to be as rare as the dodo bird; moreover,
he asserted that: "Verse has become most injurious to dramatic art.
A scenic artist whose department is the drama of the present day
should be unwilling to take a verse into his mouth. It is improbable
that verse will be employed to any extent worth mentioning in the
immediate future; the aims of the dramatists of the future are almost
certain to be incompatible with it. It is therefore doomed. For art
forms become extinct, just as the preposterous animal forms became
extinct when their day was over."[1]

Ibsen's chief English disciple, George Bernard Shaw, seconded
this declaration; for he declared that the most important part of a

54

(play) is its discussion of some particular social theory. According to Shaw, the playwright, like the novelist, must become a naturalist who applies scientific, or pseudoscientific, principles to drama, just as the naturalistic novelist is often a kind of social scientist in fiction.[2] In the United States, as well as in England, verse drama lost popularity as the new naturalistic plays came into vogue. The plays which one now considers the beginnings of a superior American drama — the social dramas of Clyde Fitch and Langdon Mitchell and the problem plays of Edward Brewster Sheldon — were written in prose and owe much of their inspiration to Ibsen and Shaw. The Romantic verse tragedies which were so popular in the nineteenth century declined in popularity as poetry yielded the stage to prose.

Because of the prevalence of naturalistic in the modern theater, several critics have declared that poetic drama is either dead or dying. Joseph Wood Krutch, for instance, asserted in *The Modern Temper* (1929) that poetic tragedy was impossible because "The world of poetry, mythology, and religion represents the world as a man would like to have it, while science represents the world as he gradually comes to discover it."[3] Allen Tate claimed in 1936 that modern poets were limited to the lyric because their era had no controlling myth to regulate the conduct of all men and women: "With the disappearance of general patterns of conduct the power to depict action that is both single and complete also disappears,"[4] and the poet could only write fragments. In 1933, Edmund Wilson wrote an essay entitled "Is Verse a Dying Technique" in which he concluded that it was, and also that any attempts to revive verse drama or the epic were futile because such techniques no longer bore any relationship to people's lives.[5]

Many poet-playwrights, however, have refused to accept the death of their favorite genre. Almost all poets, including John Neihardt, want an audience; and they believe that only poetic drama can provide the verbal dimension necessary to make drama a form of literary art. Virtually all the major modern poets — Eliot, Yeats, W. H. Auden, Stevens, Williams, Frost, Lowell, E. E. Cummings, MacLeish, Robinson Jeffers, Millay — have written verse plays, many of which have been both commercial and artistic successes.

In the United States, the movement for a modern poetic drama began with the work of three friends who had known one another at college. William Vaughn Moody, Percy MacKaye, and Josephine Preston Peabody were well-educated, were saturated with the Elizabethan dramatists, and had tried to revive poetic drama by resusitating a dead past.[6] Almost seventy years before, Emerson had warned that "the English dramatic poets have Shakespearized for two hundred years,"[7] and that the time for a change had arrived; but Moody, MacKaye, Peabody, Trumbull Stickney, Madison Cawein, Cale Young Rice, and others did not heed his warning. As a result, their plays are weak, stilted, imitative, and usually dull. Not until later in the twentieth century did better poets begin to experiment with finding verse rhythms closer to the idiom of modern speech; and only then did poetic drama begin to come out of the closet where it had been since the Romantics. The recent success of Archibald MacLeish and Robert Lowell proves that audiences will accept good verse plays.[8]

John Neihardt, however, stopped writing verse drama long before poets like Eliot, MacLeish, and Lowell began to revitalize the genre. Unfortunately for him, he had followed the example of Moody's circle in the form, style, and the subject matter of his plays. This imitation was particularly unfortunate for Neihardt since he had a toughness, a knowledge of character, and an ear for language that many better educated and more genteel playwrights lacked. Though Neihardt loved the classics, he also lived among sodbusters and Indians; had he included them in his plays, American drama would have been richer for it. Though Neihardt revolted against the genteel tradition in his fiction and in his poetry, he was one of its representatives in drama. Perhaps this representation was the result of his writing in isolation, far from the New York stage. Instead of writing actable plays, he wrote static closet drama.

Neihardt's first poetic drama, *The Fugitive Glory*, is little more than a collection of lyrics, a fact which Neihardt recognized by reprinting it only once in *Man Song* (1909). This work is a three-character discussion among Satyra, The Youth, and the Dream-Gloria, and it contains very little action. The characters are allegorical abstractions for whom the reader can develop almost no sympathy. At the beginning, Youth comes to Satyra to explain that he has found a new love, Nature, who is personified in the Dream-Gloria. Old Satyra disagrees with Youth: Nature, he claims, is a false seductress:

> She seems a spirit wrought of dream and flame,
> This Nature with her drugs of bitter milk!
> Half visible, elusive, how she weaves
> The strange, alluring many-colored dream!

> How virgin-like she seems! How she can blush
> In subtle dawn-tints! With what purple gauze
> She weaves transparent curtains for her limbs
> Of maddening allurement![9]

This over-blown verse is not good dramatic language by anyone's definition, but it is typical of early twentieth-century American poetic drama. To conclude this "play," Satyra, jealous that the Youth is about to leave, stabs him; but the Dream-Gloria still triumphs over all, for Nature is eternal and all - powerful, an easy moral for a mediocre work.

Neihardt's second verse play, *The Passing of the Lion* (1909), is a marked improvement. First of all, it is a *play* with real characters and action. The verse is still overly lush, but it is often appropriate to the characters who speak it. The play is actable, although it probably deserves its present obscurity. The biggest flaw in *The Passing of the Lion* is that it requires more background knowledge than most audiences and readers possess. The play's major character is Alcibiades, the Athenian general (450 - 404 B.C.) whose selfishness helped cause his city's defeat in the Peloponnesian War. As Neihardt's play begins, he is in exile with Timander, whom he accuses of playing Delilah to his Samson:

> This purple ease, these days of sweet forgetting,
> These nights of scarlet flame, these ashen dawns,
> Washed bright again with damning vintages!
> They have subdued the genius that was mine.[10]

Yet the reader does not sympathize very much with Alcibiades because Neihardt does not dramatize either the early genius or the seduction which destroyed it. Timander scorns the regret of Alcibiades, but she then apologizes in a passionate speech which includes these lines: "I am half mad! Oh kiss me wholly so, That I may quite forget! I burn! I freeze!"[11] But this passion is only talk without action; and the reader, or the audience — since *The Passing of the Lion* is a play — does not experience these emotions. After a final defeat, Alcibiades meets the mob which murders him. As the citizens set fire to his house, Alcibiades dares them to fight like men. If Neihardt had prepared for this scene by contrasting Alcibiades's former nobility of character with his later decadence and had then shown the audience that he was a brave, flawed hero who was trying to regain his lost self-respect, the play's conclusion might have been a moving one. Instead, it is only pathetic.

Neihardt's next play, *The Death of Agrippina* (1913), has some similar scenes and another classical setting, but Nero is a more familiar character than Alcibiades. Its characters are more fully realized than those in the earlier plays, and they do assume some humanity in spite of being monsters. The play, however, is almost totally uncharacteristic of Neihardt's other work; its leading character is a mother different from all other mothers in Neihardt's stories and poems. Usually he glorifies motherhood, sometimes to the point of worship. In other poems, Neihardt goes to the classics for inspiration and for heroic patterns of action; but in *Agrippina*, all the Romans are a bad lot. The tone of the play is also unlike anything else in Neihardt, with the possible exception of a few early poems; for Neihardt, an archetypal westerner, created heroes who are direct, energetic, and healthy. *Agrippina* is downright decadent, resembling Oscar Wilde's *Salome* in its *fin-de-siècle* excess of purple passages. It is as if Neihardt had decided to write a play embodying everything he most despised in both politics and literature.

To depart so far from his normal subject matter necessitated careful research and intensive study, even to the point of ordering a rare German book, *Agrippina: Die Mutter Neros* by Adolf Stahr. From this research, Neihardt derived his concept of the title role; for Agrippina, Neihardt said, "was absolutely 'power-mad.' "[12] In her, mother-love was combined with vanity and ambition for her son. But her son's insane vanity was greater. Even though they are despicable, the characters in *Agrippina* are supremely theatrical, and Neihardt showed an understanding of theater by choosing them. Most of Shakespeare's best heroes — Hamlet, Lear, Romeo, and Cleopatra, for example — are actors who play scenes for the other characters; and, like actors they are larger-than-life persons. In Neihardt's play, both mother and son are always performing, always pretending. The historical Nero actually did appear on the stage, one more sign of his unsuitability as an emperor. This theatricality is heightened in both Nero and his mother by their insanity. The schizophrenic acts all the time.

Agrippina takes place in 59 A.D. in the imperial villa at Barae. As the curtain rises, an orgy is occurring inside; outside, Ancietus is discussing Nero's plans for assassinating his mother by sinking her ship — a clean, quick crime. Ancietus gives this good, blunt speech:

> And no brazen wound shall bleed
> Red scandal over Rome; the nosing mob
> Shall sniff no poison, Just a gulping sob
> And some few bubbles breaking on the swell —
> Then, good night, Agrippina, rest you well!
> And may the gods revamp the silly fish
> With guts of brass for coping with that dish![13]

Neihardt's language is vivid, exact, and well suited to its speaker. The couplets march swiftly along so that the longer speeches do not drag like some passages in the earlier plays.

When Nero and Agrippina enter, Nero caresses her, thus adding incest to his list of deviant activities. He recalls his love for Poppea, whom Agrippina had murdered the year before. Crazy Nero both loves and hates his mother. Meanwhile, back at the orgy, prominent Romans, who are costumed as fauns, satyrs, cupids, and other mythological figures, dance wildly. One can imagine this dance staged with scenery by Aubrey Beardsley and music by Richard Strauss; but such a scene is too much out of character for Neihardt for him to write either a sustained or a very graphic orgy scene. As a result, the action quickly shifts back to Nero's soliloquy, a shift which the reader regrets since the soliloquy is not nearly so interesting as the orgy. Nero's insane posturing bores after a while, for he is neither subtle nor intelligent enough to sustain the audience's interest in his insanity. When Nero sees Agrippina in a colorful nightmare that same night, Neihardt's attempt at the sensational is almost ludicrous. Nero implores what he thinks is his mother's ghost:

> O — O — begone, blear thing! — She is not dead!
> You are not she — my mother! — Ghastly head —
> Trunkless — and oozing green gore like the sea,
> Wind-stabbed! Begone! Go — do not look at me —[14]

This Gorgon, however, is not dead; she is only dampened by her unexpected swim. Thus Nero has to murder her again, this time by sending Ancietus to cut her throat. As he stabs her, the lights go out; the play ends. Despite its decadent sensationalism, *Agrippina* is a promising start since the play moves well and since its characters have genuine dramatic life. Its major flaw, perhaps, is that its subject matter is not Neihardt's true material; and, as a result, one cannot sympathize with the characters.

Neihardt's last play, *Eight Hundred Rubles* (1913), is a brief parable in dramatic form about one of his favorite themes — greed and its effects. This theme appears throughout the poems and short stories, and it is also a major theme in Neihardt's two early novels *The Dawn Builder* and *Life's Lure*. In this little play, a gentle, innocent girl offers hospitality to a tramp, who rewards her with a gold piece from a sack he carries. When the girl's mother and father return home from a hard day of peasant labor, they berate her for her generosity until they hear about the gold. Then the mother begins to plot; and, while the father and daughter are gone, she takes a knife and stabs the sleeping stranger. At that moment, the father returns from the tavern with the news that the stranger tramp is really their long-lost son. Throughout the play, the mother's actions and opinions are contrasted with those of her daughter, a combination Pippa-Pollyanna who believes in the uplifting power of religion. This sentimentality destroys *Eight Hundred Rubles*, for the characters are bloodless abstractions whose actions are completely predictable. This play also indicates the unevenness of Neihardt's work at this stage of his career. By 1913 he had begun work on *A Cycle of the West*, which was to earn him a deserved reputation as an important poet; and he had also completed his excellent memoir of a trip down the Missouri, *The River and I*. Yet, in spite of his new-found artistic skill, he still occasionally indulged in sentimentality and in simplemindedness.

II *The Short Stories*

This same unevenness is also evident in Neihardt's many short stories, most of which were written before he began to concentrate on his epic poetry. These stories, collected in *The Lonesome Trail* (1907) and in *Indian Tales and Others* (1926), range from sentimental parables, prose equivalents of *Eight Hundred Rubles*, to brilliant "impressions of life." Although Neihardt's stories were popular with editors and were published in such leading magazines as *Smart Set*, he still regarded himself as primarily a poet. In fact, he resisted the flattery of one particularly persistent editor who wrote to him asking, "When are you going to give us another short story? No one can write the kind you can write."[15] After 1912, Neihardt devoted almost all his writing time to *A Cycle*. In fact, some of the stories are themselves part of his preparation for his epic poem since they treat the same themes.

The Lonesome Trail begins with Neihardt's most popular tale,

"The Alien," in which a fur trapper makes a pet of a she-wolf and then is killed by her and her mate. "The Alien" resembles the stories of Jack London and Frank Norris in which man is stripped of his social and intellectual pretensions and becomes like the beasts. In "The Alien" and in many other stories, Neihardt demonstrates what happens to men who are cast out of civilized society. Some find hope and learn to feel at home under the stars; but others, crazed by their loneliness, are reduced to complete savagery. Neihardt's main character is often a man alone in a hostile wilderness who must wage a bitter, perhaps impossible, struggle against nature or against another man. In his struggle for survival, this protagonist either affirms his humanity and becomes truly heroic or denies it and becomes like the wolves who lie in wait for him. In his better stories, Neihardt — like London, Norris, and Stephen Crane — is a naturalistic writer who expresses universal truths about human nature. Like Norris, he is concerned with the ultimate value of man's struggle; for, though an individual may fail, the Life Force of the race is imperishable. When Neihardt's fiction fails, it is chiefly because he sentimentalizes this struggle between the humane and the animalistic and converts tragedy into melodrama.

"The Alien," for example, begins with Antoine, a half-breed horse thief and murderer, in flight from his pursuers. Wounded, he finds refuge in a cave; but he must fight a female wolf to keep his den. At the first bite from her fangs, "all that was human in him passed," because "in his blood the primitive beast had grown large through long years of lonesome hiding from his kind."[16] Antoine wins his fight; but, in a gesture of forgiveness, he shares a rabbit with the wolf, which he christens "Susette" after a girl he once loved and whose father he had killed for opposing their marriage. For the second time in his life, Antoine now receives something like love from another creature; but Neihardt, to his credit, knows the wilderness too well to oversentimentalize an already incredible story. Susette leaves Antoine for a mate of her own kind, and Antoine is once again reduced to a brute as he fights the male wolf for his "bride." All his humanities disappear, history vanishes, and "from the long-slumbered dust of the prehistoric cave-man came a giant spirit to steel the sinews of its far-removed and weaker kin."[17] Just as Antoine seems about to win, Susette herself attacks him; "and the man was an alien" once more. One can imagine the effect such a story would have on a magazine reader hungry for vicarious excitement. Though it seems ordinary enough today, in fact a cut below Jack London's similar stories, it created a sensation, and editors begged Neihardt for others just like it. He refused to become a hack, however, and followed his own literary creed.

Another alien is Half-a-Day, the central character in an Indian tale entitled "The Look in the Face." Half-a-Day goes on a hunt with his friend and rival-in-love, Black Dog. In a fit of jealousy, Black Dog steals away with their food and horses, leaving his friend to die in the wilderness, just as Hugh Glass's comrade deserts him in Neihardt's *The Song of Hugh Glass.* Like Hugh Glass, Half-a-Day survives, returns to shame Black Dog in the eyes of the village; and marries Paezha, the woman they both love. Enraged, Black Dog kills Paezha and then flees. Half-a-Day hunts him down, just as Frank Talbeau hunts down Mike Fink in Neihardt's *The Song of Three Friends;* but, instead of taking vengeance, he releases Black Dog and gives him his own bow and arrows. He does so because of the piteous look in Black Dog's face, a look he once had seen in the face of Paezha. As he explains it, "I grew soft. There was a great springtime in my breast. The ice was breaking up."[18]

Like all of Neihardt's Indian tales, "The Look in the Face" uses a framing technique. An "I" who is sympathetic toward and interested in the Indian characters asks one of them to tell him a story. After it is over, the white narrator often analyzes it and tries to draw a moral. Neihardt wants to show his white readers that the actions of his Indian characters reveal important human truths and that, instead of being simple primitives, these Indians actually have a sophisticated moral and ethical philosophy. At the end of "The Look in the Face," for example, the narrator asks Half-a-Day, "Do you think Black Dog was all a coward. . . . Perhaps he only loved too much." The Indian replies, "I do not know . . . I only know sometimes I wish I had not seen that look upon his face."

The narrator of these tales is clearly not a literary persona but Neihardt himself. He spent much time among the Indians listening to their stories of the good old days, and something in those stories awakened a responsiveness in him that made him want to pass them along. Neihardt, however, did not simply record these stories as they were told to him. He was an artist not an anthropologist, and he never carried a tape recorder. Instead, he transformed these Indian tales by heightening their intensity and by creating a literary language of his own which could capture the spirit of the original Sioux or Omaha or of a literal English translation. He did this work by eliminating verbosity and disorganization and by emphasizing the symbolic and metaphorical patterns inherent in Indian speech. Neihardt, who refined this method over a thirty-year period, achieved near perfection in *Black Elk Speaks* and in his fine novel *When the Tree Flowered.*

Those tales which do not use a white narrator to provide an introductory frame are generally less effective, for in them Neihardt loses artistic perspective and cannot analyze his materials. In the frame stories, the action appears to the reader like something which happened long ago and which assumes the status of a myth that is encrusted by successive layers of meaning that are waiting to be peeled back to reveal fundamental truth. A myth, according to Elizabeth Drew's definition, is a fiction which reveals a psychic fact,[19] and these stories, at their best, do exactly that. Neihardt also uses the same technique in some of the "white" stories in which the narrator hears the fable from an old frontiersman.

In "The Scars," a good example of such a frontier story, an old trapper sits by a warm stove and tells of his trips from St. Louis to Fort Pierre as an expressman for the American Fur Company. Such trips up and down one thousand wild miles are the subject of many Neihardt works in which they are often equated with the epic voyages of the ancient Argonauts. On one such trip, so the old frontiersman recalls, he was ordered to escort a condemned murderer to St. Louis for his execution — over a thousand miles by muleback. When Neihardt has the frontiersman remember a story which this criminal had told him, he creates a double frame. In this story, two friends, Jacques and Narcisse, both love the trader's half-breed daughter, Paulette. They cut cards for her, and Narcisse wins. Later when they are out on trail together, Narcisse breaks his leg; and Jacques pretends to go for help but never returns. Here again, as in *Hugh Glass,* a man is deserted by his best friend.

Narcisse, however, is rescued; and, upon his return, he finds that Jacques is enjoying himself with Paulette. Narcisse, like Half-a-Day of "The Look in the Face," pardons his former friend; but this time the friend is ungrateful. Jacques snarls, "Why in hell didn't you die," and stabs Narcisse to finish what he had failed to accomplish by deserting his trusting comrade. Narcisse cannot forgive two sins: "And then Narcisse somehow forgot the long trails they'd tramped together and the starvings and the freezings together. Couldn't think of anything but the sting of the knife and the trickle of the blood."

He kills Jacques and is sentenced to hang.

But "The Scars" has a trick ending. The expressman lets his prisoner go, knowing that *he* is Narcisse.

> "When did I have my cap off?" said he.
> "You have a good mule there," continued I, evading his question. "You have grub, a gun and ammunition. Why don't you go west?"
> "Why are you saying that?" he said.
> "Because," I answered, "because I have seen *both scars!*"

This sort of moral fable is characteristic of Neihardt's stories, and oftentimes these fables are quite effective because the moral is dramatized, not preached. Two such fables are about Indian-white marriages which fail because the two people cannot resolve their cultural differences. In "Vylin," a father brings his daughter before the tribal elders for judgment. Long ago, she had married a white man who had played "a thing of wood and sinew," but the woman did not understand her husband's passion for his instrument: "But more and more I learned that it was no box of wood, but a living thing. For I began to see that it had the shape of a woman. Its neck was very slender; its head was small; and its hair fell down in four little braids across its neck and breasts down its hips." Because of jealousy, the woman seized a knife and killed Vylin, a crime for which her husband has deserted her and their baby and for which she is now standing judgment. "She has killed the singing spirit that the white man loved," says her father. The judges, however, are wise men who answer only that "The heart of a woman is a strange thing; who shall judge it?"

A companion story to "Vylin," but perhaps one too unbelievable and overemotional, is "Mignon," in which a strange woman of "Pars," a prostitute perhaps, attaches herself to the Wild West performer Yellow Fox. Neihardt does not relate her motives, and her actions are difficult to believe. When he returns home, Yellow Fox dreams only of Mignon; and a woman from his own people fails to ease his heartbreak. Suddenly, out of nowhere, Mignon appears; and they are happy together until Mignon tires of him. Just as soon as Yellow Fox grows angry at her and tells her to return to Paris, she becomes so submissive that she almost promises him a baby. That very night Yellow Fox awakens to find her bloody body beside him, for his Indian wife had sneaked into the teepee and killed her. In this story, the moral fable degenerates into moralistic melodrama.

Another of Neihardt's major concerns that appears in his short stories is his interest in the supernatural that began with his youthful vision that started him on a poetic career and that continued throughout his life. The theme of his poem "The Ghostly Brother" (discussed in Chapter 1) occurs several times in the stories but in "The Red Roan Mare" in particular. This story takes place during the Battle of Little Big Horn and the skirmishes that follow it. It begins with the narrator's profession of skepticism, "It's all very well to laugh at what you can't understand, and there's no defense against laughter"; but this skeptic's mind is changed when he meets Jim Dolan and Dolan's best friend, William George, the owner of the mare of the title.

Like so many men in Neihardt's stories, Dolan and George are not only close friends but also rivals in love. George is killed in battle; Dolan makes him a deathbed promise not to take the girl they both love; but Dolan, who cannot resist her, quickly breaks his oath. Later, when Dolan and the narrator are both back fighting the Sioux, Bill George's red roan mare suddenly appears. The narrator provides a rational explanation, but Dolan is deeply troubled and imagines that George's ghost has returned. Then in the heat of battle, the narrator sees the ghostly brother as Jim Dolan is shot. " 'One moment so — and with a shriek of pain the mare was off, headed for the mouth of the *arroyo*, her neck stretched out, her ears laid back — a gaunt image of sinewy speed; while Jim rolled loosely in the saddle, and the other — one with Jim from the saddle down and one with him at the hands — crossing low to the tossing mane as one who rides a race.' " The vision vanishes in a moment, but the narrator has a new opinion of the supernatural.

A similar story is "Beyond the Spectrum," in which Frank Steel, an exceptionally intelligent friend of the narrator, tries to deny his own mortality. In appearance, Steel resembles Edgar Allen Poe's Roderick Usher, and his interests are somewhat similar. Although Neihardt once spoke of how he sometimes felt the spiritual and intellectual influence of ancient Greece on his poetry and his philosophy, he has Steel want to return literally, to step beyond the spectrum, to transcend his body. As Steel puts it, " 'What if we should find within that portion of ourselves which is a child of the Infinite a latent sense not limited to a certain number of vibrations per second? . . . For us no longer the pages of the poets, and Homer's songs would be forgot. For we ourselves could stand in dread-hushed Aulis and feel the ominous silence of the windless sea!' " Steel also has another oddity: he talks to a white cat, perhaps a ghostly brother from another world. The cat answers him in musical purrs which in-

clude something that sounds like "Cleo." Late one night, the
narrator hears a terrible noise; and, when he goes to investigate, he
feels as if he too has stepped beyond the spectrum. The next day
both Steel and his cat have disappeared, but they have left a set of
mysterious, half-illegible notes about Cleo (patra?) and other
historical personages.

When Neihardt's interest in the supernatural caused him to write
ghost stories, the results were not particularly noteworthy. He lacked
the capability to portray the macabre or the unusual, and his horror
stories are only mildly titillating. When his interest in man's infinite
longings led him to the vision-quest of Sioux or Omaha, however,
the result is his finest work. Neihardt's best short story, "The Singer
of the Ache," is about such a quest for supernatural power. This excellent tale stands first in order and in rank in *Indian Tales and
Others* and develops neihardt's most characteristic theme — man's
dream and his struggle to realize it, together with the poet's isolation
and the price he must pay for his talent. Like many other stories, it
uses the frame technique to provide artistic distance and to give its
action the status of myth.

The story begins with the narrator speaking to his "White
Brother." The narrator is an old Omaha, doubtless modeled after
someone that Neihardt had met while he was working for an Indian
trader. This old man explains that his story is different, that it requires special understanding; and he warns his listener that "it is not
for you, unless you also have followed the long trail of hunger and
thirst — the trail that leads to no lodge upon the high places or the
low places, by flowing streams or where the sand wastes lie." This
formulaic introduction enhances the magical atmosphere of the story
and serves to lift it above the ordinary folk tale.

"The Singer of the Ache," says the old narrator, was a young man
named Moon-Walker, "he who walked for the moon." Once he was
an ordinary young brave, playing among the lodges, but then it
came time for him to dream. Like Black Elk and Eagle Voice in other
Neihardt stories, Moon-Walker was sent to seek his vision, to dream
the dream which would determine the course of his life — a common
experience in Plains Indian culture, but one which always fascinated
Neihardt. Perhaps he identified this practice of seeking a guiding vision with his own strange dream, a dream which, he claimed,
awakened his own sense of poetic power. After the Indian boy
receives his vision, he knows his destiny; and, by knowing it, he
becomes a man who dedicates his life to realizing his dream, just as

Neihardt dedicated his life to poetry. When he received his vision, Neihardt was delirious with fever; the Sioux and Omaha boys in his stories are often faint from fasting; but Neihardt believed nevertheless in the legitimacy of the vision that both he and they received.

Instead of seeing in his vision the usual totemic animal or battle scene, Moon-Walker sees a face, the face of the Woman of the Moon; and he returns ecstatic to his parents: " 'Oh, never have I seen so fair a face; and there was something hidden as swift as lightning; something that would be thunder if it spoke, and also there was something kind as rain that falls upon a place of heat. Into the north it looked, high up to where the lonesome star hangs patient.' " Like the young protagonists of Keats's "Endymion" and Shelley's "Alastor," the young man has looked upon a thing of beauty which becomes a joy forever; but, as it does in the Romantic epics, this experience exacts a high price — the terrible emptiness left behind when the vision fades.

Since Moon-Walker's parents are skeptical about what he has told them, they send him out again; but the Woman of the Moon again stands before him, and the vision again fades just as he reaches to hold her in his arms. His parents wonder what will become of a boy who dreams such things: "And they said: 'This is not a warrior's dream, nor is it the dream of a Holy Man; nor yet is it the vision of a mighty bison hunter. Some strange new trail this boy shall follow — a cloudy, cloudy trail!' "

The trail Moon-Walker follows is the longest and most difficult trail of all — the trail of a poet, a singer of strange songs, a singer of the ache inside. Because he seeks a vision beyond the comprehension of ordinary people, because he goes to the mountaintop, the poet is isolated, "and thus it was with the Singer of the Ache. He grew tall even to the height of a man — yet was he no man. For little did he care to hunt, and the love of battles was not his. Nor did he look upon the face of any maiden with soft eyes." His people consider him to be a fool, but he continues singing about the ache inside himself, about the terrible drive to seek immortal love and beauty regardless of the cost.

The Singer rides out alone into the wilderness, like a prophet seeking God, and he mortifies his flesh to discover spiritual truth. At last he gives up his fruitless search, finds a good woman, and settles down into Omaha domesticity; but the ache still returns. A true poet cannot resist his calling any more than a prophet can. "And after a

while the dream came back and brought the singing. Less and less
he looked upon the woman and their children. Less and less he
sought the bison, until at last Hunger came into that lodge and sat
beside the fire."

Because he does not, indeed cannot, accept his civic and familial
responsibilities, the village casts Moon-Walker out to wander in the
lonely North. But his suffering is finally rewarded. Out of his
struggle to express his vision of the true and beautiful, an immortal
poet is created: "But lo! many seasons passed and yet he lived and
was among all peoples! For often on hot dusty trails weary men sat
down to sing his songs; and women, weeping over fallen braves,
found his songs upon their lips. And when the hunger came his
strange wild cries went among the people. And all were comforted!"

"The Singer of the Ache" is a completely successful short story,
and it demonstrates Neihardt's fictional technique at its best. It contains both a convincing character portrait and a symbolic action
which reveals fundamental truths about the writer's vocation. Its
portrait of the artist is a Romantic one, shared by many nineteenth-
century poets; for Moon-Walker is one version of Emerson's ideal
bard, "He hears a voice, he sees a beckoning."[20] This kind of seeing
was Neihardt's goal, and he wrote often of its difficulty. Moon-
Walker has the same relationship to his skeptical, conformist village
that Neihardt had to the audience of Nebraska legislators present at
his laureate address. Though Neihardt was never cast out of his
home town, he never made much money, and he never won the
Pulitzer Prize. A man with high artistic standards must be willing to
suffer unpopularity. Finally, like Moon-Walker, Neihardt has been
rediscovered, and *his* songs in *A Cycle of the West* now enlighten or
inspire thousands.

Neihardt's short stories were generally well reviewed when they
first appeared, although some genteel critics reacted against them
the same way they had reacted against the work of Stephen Crane
and other naturalistic writers of the late nineteenth century. The
New York *Times,* for instance, accused Neihardt of a lack of
restraint; and one lady reviewer wrote about his stories that,
"Despite their undeniable charm and the vivid manner in which
they picture the life of the Indian and the half-breed trapper of the
west, they leave a distinctly depressing effect on the mind."[21] By
1926, when Neihardt's collected stories appeared, however, the
genteel tradition was passing, and critics no longer demanded that
literature express only the conventional and comforting aspects of
life. As a result, Neihardt's stories received a fairer reading; and the

New York *Times* called the stories "distinguished." Their critic wrote that "added to the vividness of the narrative, there is a certain beauty, a certain insight into the deeper places of the human spirit, which is all too rare in recent literature."[22] After almost fifty years, the best stories still merit this judgment.

III   *The Novels*

Neihardt's first two novels, *The Dawn Builder* and *Life's Lure*, are not as successful as his stories. The short story form forces him to concentrate his ideas and to embody them in realistic characters, just as poetry forces him to concentrate and to find metaphors for symbolizing abstract thought. But the looser novel form allows him to ramble, to moralize in long asides; and, instead of realizing the ideal, the early novels too often idealize the real. Whenever Neihardt attempts a profound philosophical statement in these books, he both generalizes and sentimentalizes to the point of boring or even embarrassing a contemporary reader. When he returned to the novel forty years later, however, he had learned to overcome these flaws. As a result, the later *When the Tree Flowered* is a major work of literary art by anyone's standards.

Neihardt's first novel, *The Dawn-Builder* (1910), begins as an enjoyable frontier yarn; but it later degenerates into something quite different. In this story, set in the year 1862, a Nebraska small-town newspaper, desperate because of the wartime manpower shortage, hires the one-eyed, peg-legged printer Waters. Neihardt, like Mark Twain, knew the print shop well from his ownership of the Bancroft *Blade*. The first section of *The Dawn-Builder* is strongly reminiscent of Twain with its boy-man friendship, its buried treasure, and its authentic Western speech. Waters is a wonderful character, colorful, original, and full of life, in spite of his several afflictions. As Neihardt describes him, "The man had but one eye. A pitiful growth of short, sandy hair straggled down his cheeks, and flared up into the semblance of dying flame where the scrubby moustache gathered in bristles above a sensitive mouth, quivering at the corners, and with lips dried and parched as with long use of stimulants."[23] Waters' helper in the print shop is young Henry Sprangs, a widow's boy who brings him whiskey when his stomach turns to "Sahary." Waters, another of Neihardt's lonely men, is isolated by his ugliness, and liquor is his only solace. After Waters slakes his physical and metaphysical thirsts, he tells young Sprangs, "I kin feel the verd're a-grow' all over my arid trac's . . . the birds is beginnin' to 'twitter in my head."

But the situation is to improve for Waters because upriver from Fort Calhoun lies buried treasure, a sunken cargo of whiskey, which Sprangs helps Waters to recover. Together they found the Buried Treasure Buffet; and, as this saloon prospers, Waters begins to dream of marrying the Widow Sprangs, a good, hearty pioneer woman. He orders a new cork leg, and then he tries to play the hero by walking to Omaha in a blizzard to fetch a doctor for Mrs. Sprangs, who has taken ill. On this heroic quest, his character assumes a new dimension: "Suddenly something out of the great white spaces went into his blood and shook him like a strong wind. It was the spirit of magnificent Defiance, the spirit that sleeps in all sublimity, in the immensity of the ocean, the vastness of prairies, the magnitude of mountains. He heard the Cry of the Epic."

"But the epic cry — it had dwindled into village gossip" as Waters's heroic quest ends on his own doorstep. Lost in the storm, he wanders in a circle. And to dash his dream completely, Bill Sprangs, the widow's long-lost husband, returns to her. Throwing away his cork leg, Waters leaves town and takes back his old job as a steamboat crewman. And at this point the structure of *The Dawn-Builder* breaks apart. The character of the novel changes completely because Neihardt's unfortunate tendency toward literary dilation — demonstrated in the passage on the epic cry — takes over. From a frontier yarn told with high spirit, an ear for speech, and an eye for description, the novel becomes a fuzzy, silly meditation on mythology and philosophy.

On a voyage upriver, Waters gets drunk; and the captain puts him ashore at One Man's Island, home of Ambrose Ambrosen and his mysterious daughter. Ambrose Ambrosen is a crazy old man with a "head like Zeus" who plays at being God. He has spent a lifetime trying to discover a sort of Life Force which holds the universe together and which has been variously personified as Jove, Brahm, Osiris, and other deities. Waters's job is to build a harp on which Ambrosen can strike "the mystic chord of seven strings" which will unlock the secret of the universal force. As for Ambrosen's daughter, Neihardt introduces her with an abysmal attempt at comedy, for he has Waters ask,

"Who's manufacturin' the biscuits?"
"Oh cook, Diana."
"Dinah, eh?" queried Waters, "colored, ey? Make good cooks — them niggers!"

Diana is absolutely perfect, a vestal virgin in the wilderness; and she awakens Waters's latent sensitivity since there is nothing like a good woman to reform a drunk. Their marriage is performed by a visiting steamboat captain to the music of "Annie Laurie" on the pilot's violin, and Diana's crazy father lurks just out of sight. The captain is also a sentimental word-painter of the most noxious sort: " 'And now, in this vast, green sanctuary of God, with the sunlight of his love about you and the dear blue of his heaven above you, I pronounce you man and wife. May the beauty of this house dwell in you hereafter. May your heart remain pure and fresh as the dew about you. In the name of Him whose spirit is the goodness and beauty of this vast wilderness, I bless you!' "

Now that the unity of the novel has been destroyed, Neihardt's loving couple leaves the island, for old Ambrosen has finally died. Waters takes Diana back to Fort Calhoun where they reside with Mrs. Sprangs, once again a widow now that her husband has disappeared forever through death. Waters thinks that he can build his rosy dawn and live happily with his forest sprite. The ways of civilization, however, are strange to Diana; and, after she bears Waters a daughter, she pines away, dies in a maudlin scene, and leaves her husband to start life all over again.

One would like to say that Neihardt's second novel, *Life's Lure* (1914), is an improvement and shows promising development, but one cannot. Even the good frontier yarn that sustained the first portion of *The Dawn-Builder* is missing. The novel is an unfortunate combination of Frank Norris's *McTeague* and of Bret Harte's "The Outcasts of Poker Flat." Its theme concerns inordinate desire for wealth, like many of Neihardt's stories and poems; but it is belabored in this novel to the point of excruciating boredom.

The plot of *Life's Lure* is an involved melodrama in which Drake, an intellectual greenhorn in the Dakota gold rush, is befriended by the urbane, civilized gambler Louis Devlin, who encourages him to give up his useless search for gold and to join a saloon business that Devlin thinks will be more profitable than any mine. When Mrs. Drake, a pretty spendthrift, comes West to join her husband, Devlin seduces her and then leaves her to die of hunger, exposure, and a broken heart; Drake then obtains revenge by drowning Devlin in a mine shaft. A subplot involves another young greenhorn from Indiana named Punkins, who falls in love with Placer Nell, a saloon girl with a heart of gold. They marry and have a child, but Punkins is forced into the wilderness for stealing gold from Monte Joe, Placer

Nell's former sweetheart. Meanwhile, all the characters are looked after by kindly Mrs. Wolliver and her lover, Pete.

As the novel begins, Drake, a sensitive intellectual who moralizes about everything, much to the detriment of the story, is about to lose his savings in a poker game. Before he can place his final bet, however, Neihardt interrupts to read his mind:

> Hope, like a lamp flame about to succumb to a draught too strong, flares big before it dies. The whirlwind glory that clings about the world's last ditches seized Drake. Of course he would win! Fate may torture a man — but in the end, she is a woman. Fear and anxiety fled; the whirlwind glory lifted him. He had not looked at the cards he had drawn — but why should he? They were just what they were! Seeing the face of fate in no way mitigates the doom. On then! One terrific plunge![24]

Much of *Life's Lure* is written in this vein, with very little comic relief. Even the Western setting seems unrealistic, perhaps because Neihardt was less familiar with the Dakota gold rush than he was with the Missouri River life that he describes in *The Dawn-Builder*.

After Drake loses the fateful card game, he has a vision in which his wife back home is waiting for the fortune he has promised her. He hears music: "O Clarinet, and there shall be June madness! Green boughs shall burst into a pink and white flame of bloom! See! her warm glowing arms are lifted for wings! Quick! One gust of melody! She smiles upon you, O Violins! For what can they be waiting — can it be for the music of Yesterday?"

Neihardt is for some reason incapable of writing a love scene without indulging in this sort of maudlin prose. Whenever he writes of white women, he resorts to a ladies' magazine style that is totally out of character for him. Perhaps he admired women too much, or perhaps he believed too literally in the old chivalric ideals. Whatever the reason, when a white woman enters, he is usually seized with an irresistible urge to elevate her into a goddess of love and beauty; and even the saloon girls in *Life's Lure* are awarded the same treatment. An excellent example of this excessive sentimentality occurs when Mrs. Wolliver, the kindly keeper of a boardinghouse, sews for Placer Nell's baby and holds up her handiwork for Pete, her rough-and-tumble lover, to admire. Their dialogue is typical of *Life's Lure*:

> "Well, I'll be cussed! Ain't it teeny though. . . . Can't get my danged finger in the sleeve!
> "Ain't it just too sweet?" cooed Mrs. Wolliver. "There ain't anything in

this world half as much joy as makin' them little things! Sometimes I think Heaven must be a place where a whole lot of good women is makin' baby clothes forever and ever!"

One wonders how the author of *Black Elk Speaks* could ever write such a conversation, but then one remembers his nawkish lyrics about the joys of fatherhood.

Unlike most of the women, all the important male characters in *Life's Lure* are motivated by greed. As a result, they all come to unfortunate ends. Punkins, for example, carries a heavy sack of gold dust for countless bitter, suffering miles without water only to discover that the sack contains only powdered yellow mica. When he returns to Bear Gulch, he sees Placer Nell in the act of refusing Monte Joe; and, misreading her character, Punkins thinks she has been untrue. Distraught, she hangs herself; and, because she leaves the baby to Mrs. Wolliver, the latter closes her boardinghouse and leaves town with Pete: "So it happened that the Boss Eating House suspended business. And one morning in midsummer, a curious procession passed up the hill and out of Bear Gulch forever. It consisted of a man, a burro, a woman, and a baby. The woman, with the baby in her arms, rode the burro. The man led."

After the debacle of *Life's Lure*, one is grateful to Neihardt for not writing any more novels until after the completion of *A Cycle of the West*. When he returned to fiction, he was no longer the unsure young man who was experimenting with different genres in an attempt to find his true voice. Instead, he was at the height of his artistic powers and was in complete control of both his method and his material. His last novel, *When the Tree Flowered* (1951), is a work of excellent craftsmanship; and it stands third — after *A Cycle of the West* and *Black Elk Speaks*, which deal with the same subjects — in a ranking of his books.

Subtitled *An Authentic Tale of the Old Sioux World*, *When the Tree Flowered* has the same technique that Neihardt uses in his Indian tales. In fact, it resembles a collection of short stories because each chapter is a complete episode which can stand alone. The narrator is an old Sioux named Eagle Voice, who lectures to a young white man, the "I" of the novel, about the way things used to be when the great tree of the Sioux nation was in flower. Eagle Voice is a composite character who bears considerable resemblance to Black Elk, but he is based especially on Eagle Elk, an Ogalala Sioux who died in 1945 after living more than ninety years and who could have taken part in many of the events described in the novel.[25] Many of the scenes in this book also appear in *Black Elk Speaks*, for Black Elk gave Neihardt hundreds of pages of material, not all of which were used in the earlier book.

As in the stories, Neihardt's use of an Indian narrator, who tells his story to a white listener, enables him to gain the artistic distance and the detachment which the two early novels certainly lack. The narrator's point of view also provides the author with control of the action without his intervening directly in it. When one episode ends, Eagle Voice simple says that he is tired; to begin again, the listener comes to his cabin and asks for another story. The listener becomes a very close friend of Eagle Voice, almost like a son, just as Neihardt became like a son to Black Elk. *When the Tree Flowered* begins with a description of the one-room cabin on Pine Ridge Reservation, home of the Oglala after their defeat; and the landscape is one of utter poverty and desolation. Their present desolation is contrasted to their past glory throughout the novel. The feeble old man who was once the epitome of physical development, now has only his spirit left, and it is rapidly fading. Yet an intense pride remains, as Eagle Voice explains, "But it is only my body that stoops, remembering the mother ground . . . for I can feel my spirit standing tall above all the snows and grasses that have been, and seeing much of good and evil days."[26]

Here, and throughout the novel, Neihardt does with Eagle Voice and his Sioux friends what J. M. Synge did with the Aran Islanders: he transforms their speech patterns into poetry. *When the Tree Flowered* is not simply a stenographic record such as an anthropologist might record; it is a transformation into art by concentration and heightening. Neihardt had heard doubtlessly the stories Eagle Voice tells from the Sioux, but they did not write the novel for him. He selected, edited, shaped, invented, and changed details to suit his own artistic purposes. A writer's source is not nearly so important as the way in which he uses it. Holinshed's *Chronicles* and the Old French *fabliaux* are of little importance in themselves, but their transformations by Shakespeare and Chaucer are artistic, as is the case with *When the Tree Flowered*.

Eagle Voice begins his story with a brief description of the old Sioux way "before the hoop of our people was broken." Neihardt places this description first because the integrity of this way of life is a central theme in the novel. In contrast to the diversity of twentieth-century life, the Sioux were as unified as Henry Adams's cathedral builders. Each person had his or her proper position; but, unlike the feudal peasant, each Sioux was treated as an individual; and the Sioux had both individual freedom and collective security. Even in the most severe winters, few Sioux ever starved, for the rich gained honor by giving to the poor, and the strong were praised when they hunted not for themselves but for the weak.

Even the old Indians had a form of social security: " 'Maybe a man was so bent and stiff that he could not hunt or fight any more and maybe he could hardly chew his meat; but he had happy work to do, because there were always little boys who had to learn how to be good hunters and brave warriors; and he would teach them and tell them stories that were teaching too.' " The symbol of this unity was the sacred hoop that encircled the nation, and it is also the central symbol in *Black Elk Speaks.* When this hoop was broken by the white man, the unity was destroyed; and the living tree, symbol of the Nation's living spirit, withered and died.

Eagle Voice's father was killed defending the great hoop against the white man; but, even after the early battles, the nation was still intact. Eagle Voice's father was carried to a hilltop scaffold, and there the boy heard him speak and saw a heaven filled with buffalo. Wakan Tanka, the Great Spirit, keeps his warriors safe, and life goes on within the hoop. Eagle Voice is a product of a system of child rearing that, as Neihardt describes it, is both profound and beautifully simple since it is a natural outgrowth of the Sioux way. The Sioux way is an organic, creative pattern of living; and its system of laws is designed to preserve the nation's integrity, to keep the sacred hoop intact. All must be one: "If you broke a law, it was like breaking the sacred hoop a little; and that was a bad thing, for the hoop was the life of the people all together." Because of this sense of unity, no Sioux parent ever needed to punish his children, for even they knew that they had to stay within the safety of the hoop.

Eagle Voice then describes some episodes from his childhood — chasing cow buffalo, playing war games, and otherwise preparing to be a warrior. These episodes are authentic, gay, humorous, and clever, and they seem to flow naturally from the well of Sioux experience. Finally, Eagle Voice is ready for his vision quest, the central event in the life of any Sioux boy and the subject of many other Neihardt stories and poems. After purification in a sweat lodge, he is told the story of the sacred hoop. The hoop has four quarters, and each one has its own power, which is symbolized by sacred objects and by a sacred color. By these powers the Sioux must live. The south is blue, the color of thunder, and its objects are the bow of lightning and the cup of rain. The north is white, like the snow, and its objects are the white-goose wing and a sacred herb; for it has the power of healing. The east is red for the rising sun, and its totems are the morning star and the peace pipe. The west is yellow like the summer sun, which makes things grow, and its objects are the sacred staff of six branches ("for the power of growth") and the little hoop ("for the life of the people who flourish as one"). From south to north across the hoop runs the good red road of spirit; from east to west, the black road of earthly difficulties. Where the two roads meet at the center of the hoop, the sacred Tree of Life grows and flowers; and the closest Christian equivalent to this intersection of the timeless with time is the Crucifixion, symbolized by another sort of tree. Above the hoop is Wakan Tanka; below it is Maka, Mother Earth. This picture of the world, implanted in every Sioux, symbolized the unity of life, showed him the road he must follow, and gave him a sense of belonging to his nation. The flowering tree is a lovely symbol of organic unity, of life lived in harmony with nature, of fertility, and, most of all, of hope.

With this knowledge, Eagle Voice goes out alone to seek his vision, but he has difficulties. The vision will not come to him. At long last, he sees an eagle and hears a voice which counsels him, "Hold fast to your pipe, for there is more." He also sees some coup-sticks (used to touch a dead enemy and "count coup") which foretell success in battle; but, when compared with the magnificent and elaborate vision of Black Elk, Eagle Voice's dream seems insignificant. The phrase he hears "Hold fast, there is more" seems unimportant at first, but it later assumes a much larger meaning when it symbolizes and evokes a sense of spiritual power which will last beyond earthly existence and is always a promise of greater things to come. Neihardt himself uses the phrase in this way in the last chapter of his autobiography, *All Is But a Beginning*. In the case of Eagle Voice, "more" means a second vision; and this time he sees the hoop of his nation and the flowering tree, a vision which sustains him throughout his long life because it symbolizes the physical and spiritual health of all Sioux.

Through this narrative, the character of Eagle Voice remains consistent and believable. The reader accepts his vision because Neihardt makes him believe the Indian. One sees him not as some savage fanatic but as an honest young man who is seeking a direct revelation of the truth. Because the reader believes in his vision and sympathizes with him, the loss of that vision late in the novel is all the more poignant. The fall of the Sioux nation is a tragedy which results not from an inner flaw but from outside pressure. If the Sioux are flawed in any way, it is only that they are too honest, too faithful, too trusting in their sacred hoop.

As Eagle Voice grows older, he becomes adept at both hunting and fighting; and he also becomes interested in girls. Unlike the love scenes in the first two novels, those in *When the Tree Flowered* are restrained, touching, and poetic; for the emotion is suggested rather than directly expressed. The object of Eagle Voice's affection is Tashina Wamblee; and as he remembers her in his old age, " 'Her face was all shining and she was singing to me. I cannot say what look was in her eyes. I think I did not see the look clearly until I was older and my eyes were getting tired of all I had seen instead.' "

Now a promising young warrior, Eagle Voice also participates in the famous Sioux Sun Dance in which long rawhide thongs with wooden skewers at one end are attached to a tall tree which represents the sacred flowering tree. The warriors cut slits in their chests; insert the skewers; lean back, and dance; and gaze at the top of the tree until the skewers pull themselves out or until the dancers black out from staring at the sun. In the novel, the Sun Dance does not seem like a barbaric ritual; instead, it is a way to seek a vision, to get out of one's self for a moment, and to be for one instant at the spot where the two roads meet — the intersection of the temporal and the eternal. When Eagle Voice has a momentary glimpse into the world beyond this one, he sees by an Eternal Light:

"The light was so clear that I could see their happy faces, and I knew that they were all my people. Many, many of them were glowing, and those were the ever-living ones who had died. I saw many darker ones who were still in this world, but all were united in the clear, happy day. When I looked for my father, he was there all glowing, and beside him was a young man who did not glow. When I looked harder at the young man, I could see it was myself. Then the wide land went out and I was falling, dizzy, in a darkness."

After the visions, Eagle Voice participates in the battles against George Crook and George Armstrong Custer. Eagle Voice loses his friends and watches the bison disappear. He himself is protected by a sacred quirt, given to him by a respected elder, that he carries with him always to make him invulnerable. Though Eagle Voice is still quite young, he understands what is coming in spite of the great Sioux victory on the Greasy Grass. In the novel, he recalls the suffer-

ing as the cavalry pursued the Sioux and finally forced them to give
up their futile resistance. After the battles, he has a glimpse of the
outside world while traveling with Buffalo Bill's Wild West Show to
"the village called Pars." There he meets a kind woman, one much
like the Mignon in the short story Neihardt had written forty years
earlier. But Eagle Voice's love for his nation is stronger than for the
woman — and so is his love for Tashina even though he knows that
she has married another man. When Buffalo Bill realizes Eagle
Voice's homesickness, he lets him return to his people to witness
their final death.

Back in Sioux territory, Eagle Voice finds his people gripped by
the Ghost Dance religion which has been brought to them by the
Paiute Messiah, Wovoka, whom the Sioux regard as a returned
Christ whose mission is to save them, to make the Wasichus disappear, to bring the bison back (see Chapter 5 for a more detailed
discussion). Eagle Voice realizes the desperation of this last hope.
His description of the Ghost Dance is particularly moving:

"After the big meeting, the people began dancing the sacred dance and
singing the sacred songs. They held hands and made a hoop as they danced
and sang, and at the center of the hoop there stood the *chun wakon* [sacred
tree]. It was like the sacred hoop that Blue Spotted Horse told me about
when I was a boy going on vision quest, and the tree at the center should fill
with leaves and blooms and singing birds. But the tree was dead and the few
leaves on top were dry."

The massacre at Wounded Knee Creek ends the Ghost Dance
religion. After the battle, Eagle Voice finds his old love, Tashina
Wamblee, huddled under a blanket and holding the dead body of
her little boy. Her husband is dead, and Eagle Voice takes his place
until Tashina herself dies, many years later. To ease the pain of his
remembrance, the old man blows on his eagle-bone whistle. The
narrator asks,

"Grandfather, you still have your eagle-bone whistle; but what became of
the sacred quirt?"
    Slowly he returned to awareness of my presence, the smile and glow warm
upon his time-carved face.
    "When she died —" he said in a low gentle voice that quavered a bit —
"when she died, I just put it down beneath her dress, between her breasts. I
would not need it any more."

When the Tree Flowered is a successful novel by any critical standards, and it was universally praised when it was first published. Poet Paul Engle, for example, praised Neihardt's "supple and solid prose," but he was even more impressed by the book's sense of values and by its understanding of Indian life.[27] Oliver La Farge, author of *Laughing Boy*, the best-known novel of American Indian life, was equally impressed. He wrote that "the narrative of Eagle Voice *per se* is warm, human, and humorous, and without overwriting contains many passages of the really fine writing one hopes for in the prose work of a good poet."[28] In spite of these excellent reviews, *When the Tree Flowered* has received little attention until recently; but, since it is now available in paperback, more people may discover the extent of Neihardt's achievement.

Rich in both character and incident, the style of the novel is restrained, dignified, and poetic. All the climax of his long writing career (climax, that is, until he began to work on his autobiography), Neihardt demonstrated the mastery he had achieved after forty years of work with the same material. By having Eagle Voice tell his story in his own words, Neihardt is able to repeat the success of *Black Elk Speaks* with the extra advantage of being able to invent details to fill out his account. Yet the reader is barely conscious of the fact that *When the Tree Flowered* is fiction because its authenticity is so complete. One believes in every character; each incident could well have happened to a young Sioux growing to maturity while his nation crumbled around him. Because Neihardt makes the reader believe so strongly in Eagle Voice, because he makes one share Eagle Voice's vision of the good life, the destruction of the Sioux nation assumes the magnitude of tragedy. The novel reveals the tragic fall of both a great man and a worthy nation. Though Eagle Voice does not seem quite so spiritual as Black Elk or as heroic as Crazy Horse, he may be a more sympathetic character than either. He is not a "noble savage"; he is a human being with human emotions, human desires, and a profound human faith in his own vision of the good life. The greatest novelist, according to Henry James, is the one who gives the reader the fullest impression of life. Judged by that standard, *When the Tree Flowered* ranks with the best American novels of the past twenty years.

CHAPTER 4

Nonfiction

JOHN Neihardt's three most important works of nonfiction —
The River and I (1910), *The Splendid Wayfaring* (1920), and
Black Elk Speaks (1932) — provided sources for his epic poem, *A Cycle of the West* (1949). In *The River and I*, Neihardt learned the
power and grandeur of the mighty Missouri and also something
about the kind of men who were brave enough to face its terrors. *The
Splendid Wayfaring* tells in prose the story of Jed Smith, which
became *The Song of Jed Smith* (1941) in *A Cycle of the West*. *Black
Elk Speaks* is the result of Neihardt's desire for firsthand information
about the Ghost Dance, but what began as research for *The Song of
the Messiah* (1935) became his best-known book. In each case,
Neihardt went beyond his original goal and created works of literary
art.

I The River and I

Neihardt's first "research project" is recorded in *The River and I*,
which began as a series of articles for *Outing Magazine*, was then
published as a book in 1910, and won considerable critical praise.
The River and I is the record of a two-thousand-mile canoe trip
Neihardt and two friends took in July of 1908, from Fort Benton,
Montana, to Sioux City, Iowa. The book recounts their adventures
and also contains Neihardt's meditations about the Missouri River's
importance to American history. To eastern readers, Neihardt's account reads like high adventure, which in fact it was; but it was
something else as well. It was the beginning of an epic, and some
critics were perceptive enough to realize what Neihardt's purpose
was. The American Library Association, for instance, called it "a
delightful outdoor book . . . making you feel that a panoramic sweep
of country properly calls for epic treatment."[1]

The epic scale of *The River and I* is evident as early as the first chapter, in which Neihardt describes how his father used to take him to see the Missouri River in flood stage. Its size and force not only excited his imagination but gave him his first "wee glimpse into the infinite."[2] When he began writing poetry, that memory returned, and the river became a favorite symbol. Like the Transcendentalists, Neihardt worked from nature to spirit; and, in the brown, swirling waters of the Missouri, he saw a hieroglyph for nature's omnipotence and another version of his most important poetic theme — the struggle to achieve a worthy goal. As he expressed its significance, the symbol ". . . is the concrete representation of the earnest desire, the momentarily frustrate purpose, the beating at the bars, the breathless fighting of the half-whipped but never-to-be-conquered spirit, the sobbing of the wind-broken runner, the anger, the madness, the laughter. And in it all the unwearying urge of a purpose, the unswerving belief in the peace of a far away ocean."

In order to use this symbol in his poetry, Neihardt had to know it. He had to learn its secrets, just as Thoreau had had to search for the long-lost bottom of Walden Pond. To make his discoveries, he had to go back in time and experience the river as the fur trappers had in the 1820s. These traders were men of epic strength and courage, which Neihardt himself had to recapture; for, "To create an epic," he wrote, "it had been said somewhere, the poet must write with the belief that the immortal gods are looking over his shoulder." Americans no longer believe in immortal gods, but they have found a substitute for that belief. In Neihardt's words, "We [Americans] have long since discovered the divinity within ourselves, and so we have flung across the continent and seas the visible epics of will."

To Neihardt, these "visible epics" were created by the fur traders; and their history "makes the Trojan War look like a Punch and Judy show!" "An epic story," he points out, "is the story of heroic men battling, aided or frustrated by the superhuman. And in the fur trade era there was no dearth of battling men, and the elements left no lack of superhuman obstacles." When Neihardt then names some of these nineteenth-century Hectors — Mike Fink, Hugh Glass, Jed Smith, Father deSmet, Rose the Renegade, J. J. Astor, Alexander MacKenzie — they are the same men that he chronicles in *A Cycle of the West*.

But before Neihardt could write this story, he had to live part of it for himself. Neihardt's trip begins at the Great Falls of the Missouri, where man's physical self is almost swallowed up. The trolley cars and peanut stands seem to disappear as Neihardt discovers the correspondence between the river and his own soul, just as Thoreau discovers a similar correspondence in *Walden*. "I saw my Titan brother as he was made — four hundred yards of writhing, liquid sinew, strenuously idle, magnificently worthless, flinging meaningless thunders over the vast arid plain, splendidly empty under sun and stars!" Neihardt is reminded of Walt Whitman, who had sought the same relationship with the natural world, the same discovery of spiritual truth. In fact, Whitman uses the ocean as a metaphor to express the infinite in much the same way as Neihardt uses the river. In "Crossing Brooklyn Ferry," Whitman asserts his metaphorical, symbolical, intellectual, and spiritual kinship with all people who ever have been or ever will be, just as Neihardt uses this Missouri voyage to assert the immortality of his own epic quest. The river is immortal, and the poet shares it with those who will follow him. His readers will share his experience, and thus be united with him.

Neihardt also shows his kinship with Whitman and other Romantic poets when he uses Emerson's theory of language, first pronounced in *Nature*.[3] Like both English and American Romantics, Neihardt reads nature symbolically. A solitary hawk or coyote has importance beyond its own existence, for it is a symbol which bridges the gap between mortal man and immortal spirit:

A hawk wheeled and swooped and floated far up in the dazzling air. Somehow that hawk seemed to make the lonely place doubly lonely. Did you ever notice how a lone coyote on a snow-heaped prairie gives you a heartache, whereas the empty waste would only have exhilarated you? Always, it seemed, that veering hawk had hung there, and would hang there so always — outliving the rising of suns and the drifting of stars and the visits of the moon.

In Neihardt's lyric poetry, his need to discover this sort of permanent spiritual truth sometimes leads him into a misty vagueness. The prose, in contrast, is refreshingly concrete because Neihardt always pulls back from meditating about the meaning of what he sees. The Missouri River cannot be successfully navigated by a dreamy poet who lets his mind soar into the empyrean. In *The River and I* is another version of Melville's famous parable in *Moby Dick* about the dreamer at the masthead; Melville warns the idealistic watchman that the terrors of the ocean await the careless Platonist. In *The River and I*, platonic idealism yields to hunger. At Fort Benton, Neihardt dreams of the old days, but he finds more satisfying pleasure in a steaming plate of lamb chops: ". . . and for a quarter of an hour, the far weird cry of things that are no more, was of no avail.

The rapid music of knife and fork drowned out the asthmatic snoring of the ghostly packets that buck the stream no more. How grub does win against centuries!"

The simple physical descriptions in *The River and I* are notable enough in themselves, and they need no long-winded philosophical explanations. Little Bull Buffalo and his friends certainly demonstrated their heartiness by traveling two thousand miles in two months in a canoe with a balky motor. They battled scorching heat, drenching rain, a strong headwind, ferocious mosquitoes, and the skepticism of almost everyone they met along the way. These people, who are remembered in a series of short character sketches, include genuine cowboys who speak colorful phrases as "day-wrangler," "night-hawks," and "war-bags" and who perform wondrous music on their mouth-organs; a camp full of Assinboines — shy pretty girls Neihardt coaxes into a photograph — and an old chief in feathers and beads; a Mandan village of mud lodges where he is scolded by an eighty-year-old squaw and pays fifty cents for a loaf of indigestible bread; a boatload of men assigned the important but thankless chore of ridding the river of snags; and a kindly rancher who demonstrates Western hospitality at its best.

And always present is the river itself — majestic, powerful, inscrutable, treacherous, muddy, wild, tame, and, above all, lovely. In spite of the towns which line her banks, the Missouri often seems as pure as she did when Lewis and Clark ascended it to chart America's new territory: "I thought of the steamboats and the mackinaws and the keel-boats and the thousands of men who had pushed through this dream-world and the thought was unconvincing. Fairies may have lived here, indeed; and in the youth of the world, a glad, young race of gods might have dreamed gloriously among the yellow crags. But surely we were the first men who had ever passed that way — and should be the last."

Neihardt's Missouri is much like Mark Twain's Mississippi, a place of peace and wonder where, as Huck Finn says, "A fellow can feel mighty free and easy and comfortable on a raft."[4] Even in a torrential thunderstorm, the river is still a beautiful thing. The Dakota Badlands Neihardt calls "The Land of Awe." Inside a stone cathedral made by river bluffs, he sights an eagle, "Jove's eagle," and gets a glimpse into eternity. In such a place, a man may discover the best in himself, as Huck does on the Mississippi. All petty affairs vanish; and, like Thoreau at Walden Pond, Neihardt is free to "front only the essential facts of life."[5] At night, beside the campfire, he discovers his true nature: "It all came back there by the smoldering

fires — the wonder and the beauty and the awe of being alive. We
had eaten hugely — a giant feast. There had been no formalities
about that meal. Lying on our blankets under the smoke-drift, we
had cut with our jack-knives the tender morsels from a haunch as it
roasted. When the haunch was at last cooked to the bone, only the
bone was left."

This passage summarizes Neihardt's main purpose in making the
long, difficult, and sometimes dangerous voyage down the Missouri.
He wanted to bind himself, across a hundred years of history, to the
fur traders who had also shared a tender haunch around an open fire.
Away from the towns and the ranches, Neihardt could experience
the wild Missouri as they knew it; and he imagines them everywhere
along the river. Old Fort Benton, he says, should be revered as an
American Acropolis, for it was there that an epic story took place.
People dig at Troy and carry guidebooks to Athens, but Fort Benton
is deserted: "And yet, one of the most tremendous of all human
movements centered about it — the movement that brought about
the settlement of the Northwest." Most people see the West as the
setting for cowboy romances but forget its more important history.

In the West, a man also faces the essentials of poetry. At Sentinel
Rock, Neihardt stares down at the deep, cold, dark-colored water
and remembers an old spring that he had haunted as a child, often
staring down into its heart of darkness: "It fascinated me in a terrible
way. I thought Death looked like that. Even now I am afraid I could
not swim long in clear waters with those fearful colors under me. I
am sure they found Ophelia floating like a ghastly lily in such a
place." *The River and I* is full of such moments, for Neihardt is trying out his literary skills on the material he was to use for the next
forty years. He is testing his literary and historical imagination to see
whether or not he can recapture the true spirit of the fur traders
about whom he wants to write, and he passes the test with high
marks.

At the end of the book, Neihardt echoes Thoreau, who went to
Walden to discover himself and create a work of art:

When I started for the head of navigation a friend asked me what I ex-
pected to find on the trip. "Some more of myself," I answered.
And, after all, that is the Great Discovery.

After such a discovery, and after such adventure, city life pales; for
"towns, after all, are machines to facilitate getting psychically lost."

In the wilderness, however, man can find his proper psychic direction and set his lifelong course by his true star.

II   The Splendid Wayfaring

Neihardt's second major work of nonfiction is also about the Missouri River and the trappers who used it as a highway to the West. *The Splendid Wayfaring*, a history of Jed Smith's explorations of the West, begins with young Smith's first trip up the Missouri in 1822 and ends with his death in the desert nine years later. The book is an analysis of Smith's character and, through him, of the other fur trappers who opened the West to settlement by discovering the important routes to California. Because it is a history, this book is less personal than *The River and I*; but Neihardt's knowledge of the river and his affection for it are still quite evident. For this reason, *The Splendid Wayfaring* was not surpassed in description of character or in literary style for thirty years. Not until the publication of Bernard De Voto's *Across the Wide Missouri* was there another history of the fur trade which so successfully combined historical scholarship and literary art.

The Splendid Wayfaring is not a comprehensive history like Hiram Martin Chittenden's *The American Fur Trade*, nor does it bristle with footnotes, although Neihardt did a good deal of research in the collections of the Missouri Historical Society and in other important sources. Neihardt was not a professional historian, but he knew that "the general mood of a given period is more important than the bare facts."[6] He took, therefore, the liberty of supplying minor details which are always consistent with both the men and their times. Instead of writing a comprehensive history, Neihardt concentrates on one man, Jedediah Strong Smith, because he believed Smith was the most remarkable of all the mountain men and explorers who opened the land route to California and Oregon.

Because Smith's life was particularly rich in both adventure and discovery, Neihardt is able to say a great deal about the mountain men, the fur trade, and the entire western movement in a relatively short and always lively book. Smith himself is a fascinating person. He was so brave, so steadfast, and so insatiable to discover what lay beyond the Rockies that it is difficult not to accuse Neihardt of writing fiction. Smith deserves a place in the pantheon of American heroes with Daniel Boone because his deeds have the same legendary quality and an equal, or perhaps even greater, historical importance. Yet Jed Smith is only a name in history books. As Neihardt points out in his preface to *The Splendid Wayfaring*, every schoolboy knows about the official government expeditions to explore the West, but he knows little about individual fur traders who actually opened the way for westward expansion.

This westward expansion is to Neihardt one of the crucial events in all of history — one as important as the fall of Troy or Rome, as important even as the discovery of America — for the American westward movement represents the final phase of a movement which began at the dawn of recorded history. The Aryan or Indo-European race, Neihardt says, began thousands of years ago to migrate westward from the Tigris and Euphrates and continued that migration until it reached the Pacific Coast in the nineteenth century.

Today the word "Aryan" recalls memories of Nazism, but for Neihardt this theory provides a coherent, unified view of all history. Instead of seeing the various empires as isolated moments in history, he regards them as different manifestations of the same phenomenon: "We might liken the ancient Aryan spirit to a prairie fire driven by an east wind out of Mesopotamia and destined to burn across a world. Now it flared up in Persia, and the gloom of the past is still painted with that flare. Now it was a white radiance in Greece, the clear illumination of which still guides the feet of men. Now it burned ruddily in Rome, spread around the Mediterranean, and became as a golden noonday to all the known world. Then it drove northward and lit Europe with a succession of illuminations."

By this interpretation, Neihardt does not mean to endorse the triumph of a master race; and his sympathetic treatment of the American Indian and his interest in Oriental philosophy should absolve him from such a charge. What he wants to communicate and preserve is the poetic, imaginative, and forceful spirit which he sees as the creative source behind the works of western civilization from the *Illiad* to the Conestoga wagon. The same spirit or need which moves men to create works of art and science also drives them over mountains, and it also drove Jedediah Strong Smith to his discoveries.

Whether or not Neihardt's theory about the nature of men who create history is true, it is an excellent one for a poet since it enables him to see the universal significance of one man's actions. These actions, he believes, are motivated by the same desires that have always motivated great men. In his introduction to *A Cycle of the West*, Neihardt speaks of the westward movement as "a genuine epic period, differing in no essential from the other great epic periods that marked the advance of the Indo-European peoples out of Asia and across Asia Europe."[7] This period, like other epic periods, was marked by "intense individualism" and by a sense on the part of many people that it was time to move once more. The Jed Smith that Neihardt depicts in *The Splendid Wayfaring* understands this motivation quite well, and Neihardt can dramatize through his story an entire historical movement, illustrating in the process the driving force behind all Western history — the need to know.

The Splendid Wayfaring begins in Cincinnati in 1822, and Neihardt's description of the riverboats, their cargoes, and their passengers resembles Homer's catalog of ships. This passage, like others in the book, is more than a simple listing. It is full of energy, the restless urge which sends these boats down the Ohio River, then up the Mississippi and Missouri. It is the first scene of a momentous drama.

Suddenly above the babble a boat horn strikes up a merry lilt. Others join in; and far away, like spirit bugles out of the dim past of the race, still sounding the westward advance, the echoes sing on among the wooded hills. With a roar from her whistle the steamboat backs out, swings round, and, thrusting her stubborn nose into the swirl, pushes on toward Pittsburgh, snoring like an asthmatic sleeper. The cumbrous barge, poled by a dozen brawny men, moves slowly outward, feels the clutch of the current, and sweeps away. The ark-like broadhorn follows, while, startled by the shouting of the men and the blaring of the horns, the geese and chickens and sheep and cows and pigs and horses add each their own peculiar cries to the general din. And, indeed, why should they not be heard? Have they not shared as comrades in the age-long adventure of the race?

This talent for making historical events come alive serves Neihardt well throughout *The Splendid Wayfaring*.

One of the eager passengers at Cincinnati is Jed Smith, who is different from the ordinary fur trader in that he has had a little education, knows some Latin, is familiar with the Scriptures, and understands, therefore, the importance of his own actions. In addition to the usual pioneer qualities of strength, endurance, and courage, Smith has an inquiring mind and an understanding of his own motives. From reading classical literature, Neihardt had learned the principle that only an extraordinary man can be a genuine epic hero; though one may sympathize with Hector and Achilles, one has no special admiration for ordinary spear carriers. Classical tragedy also deals with the fall of a great man, a king, a prince, or a general; and

Jed Smith is a prince among trappers. His death is a direct result of his overwhelming need to discover, to find the truth about the blank spaces on his maps. Though he commits no murder, he shares this relentless pursuit for truth with such tragic heroes as Oedipus and Hamlet, men who are not content to leave well enough alone. This thirst for knowledge is both man's most admirable characteristic and the cause of his downfall. From Genesis on, human beings have created trouble because they want to know.

Smith also has a sense of Christian duty, and he carries his Bible at all times. This duty tells him that he must serve his fellow man as well as he can in whatever way he can. He readily accepts every difficult assignment offered him, not out of bravado, for he was a prudent man, but because of his dedication to what he conceived to be his mission in life. Smith himself said it best in a letter that Neihardt quotes to conclude *The Splendid Wayfaring:*

"It is that I may be able to help those who stand in need that I face every danger. It is for this that I pass over the sandy plains, in heat of summer, thirsting for water where I may cool my overheated body. It is for this that I go for days without eating, and am pretty well satisfied if I can gather a few roots, a few snails, or better satisfied if we can afford ourselves a piece of horse-flesh, or a fine roasted dog; and most of all it is for this that I deprive myself of the privilege of society and the satisfaction of the converse of my friends!"

The story of this remarkable man is certainly an exciting one. *The Splendid Wayfaring* traces Smith's travels throughout the West and recounts his important discoveries, especially the land route to California. Along the way, Neihardt also tells the story of other members of the fur traders known as Ashley-Henry men — Hugh Glass and Mike Fink, for example. He describes their canoe and keelboat voyages through treacherous rapids on the Missouri, the Green, and the Colorado; and their battles against Cree, Blackfoot, and Sioux are delineated. Throughout the book runs the theme of constant struggle against the hostile country, which seems unwilling to give up its bounty of furs without a fight. In this passage, for instance, Neihardt recreates trapper Thomas Fitzpatrick's journey north from the Green to the headwaters of the Sandy River, and he brilliantly conveys the extent to which these trappers suffered:

All forenoon the ponies travelled northward at a swinging walk across a baked plain of whitish clay mixed with gravel, where even sagebrush was scarce. Then the soil became sandy, and soon the party was floundering through a wilderness of dunes where not even sagebrush grew. With drooping heads the sweating animals labored on through the thirsty land. Away to the northeast the snowclad mountains, tauntingly near to the eyes but discouragingly distant for the feet, glittered in the white glare of the day. The sun burned red over the rim of the melancholy waste, and disappeared, and the air turned chill. Night without wood or water or grass!

These same incidents and characters are also described by Neihardt in *A Cycle of the West* on which he was working while writing *The Splendid Wayfaring*. In both poetry and prose, he demonstrated that the wayfaring of Jed Smith and his compatriots was indeed splendid. His books show man at his best in his struggle to fill in the blank spaces on the map and at his worst in the struggle to survive at any cost, a struggle which sometimes turned men into animals. Hugh Glass, for instance, was left for dead after being clawed and crushed by a grizzly because the men left behind to guard his wounded body were afraid of an Indian attack. Jed Smith, however, represents the best type of frontiersman; and *The Splendid Wayfaring* gives him back to Americans.

III Black Elk Speaks

Neihardt's research about the fur trade resulted not only in *The Splendid Wayfaring* but in three epic poems: *The Song of Three Friends, The Song of Hugh Glass,* and *The Song of Jed Smith.* His research about the Sioux, which was originally intended primarily as background for *The Song of the Indian Wars* and for *The Song of the Messiah,* resulted instead in Neihardt's most popular and most enduring book, *Black Elk Speaks,* the memories of an Oglala Sioux holy man whom Neihardt first met in August, 1930. He was then writing *The Song of the Messiah,* and he wanted some firsthand information about the Ghost Dance religion of the late 1880s, which is also an important subject in *When the Tree Flowered.*[8] For that reason, he and his son Sigurd traveled to Pine Ridge Reservation in hopes of finding an old man who had witnessed the coming of Wovoka, the Paiute Messiah, who, many Indians believed, had been sent by God to save them from destruction. With help from the reservation agent, Neihardt learned about a man who lived in a one-room cabin and who was regarded as *wichasha wakon,* a holy man. When he and his son arrived at the old man's cabin, he was sitting outside, almost as if he had known the poet was coming. Then, as they sat silently appraising one another, the old Sioux, who knew no English, looked at the interpreter and spoke, "As I sit here, I can feel in this man beside me a strong desire to know things of the Other World. He has been sent to learn what I know, and I will teach him."

This meeting began a long and important friendship. The poet and the holy man corresponded all winter with the aid of Ben Black Elk, the old man's son who had studied at the Carlisle Indian school. The following May, Neihardt returned to Pine Ridge with his daughters, Enid, who acted as his secretary, and Hilda, to begin the difficult job of recording Black Elk's teachings. But Neihardt was more than a recorder, for his "function [was] to translate the old man's story, not only in the factual sense — for it was not the facts that mattered most — but rather to recreate in English the mood and manner of the old man's narrative. This was often a grueling and difficult task requiring much patient effort and careful questioning of the interpreter."[9] Neihardt also believed that his duty to be true to Black Elk was a "sacred obligation," for he was certain that "there were times when we had more than the ordinary means of conversation."

A year later, the record of these conversations, *Black Elk Speaks*, was published; and it received praise from every reviewer, including many who had not the slightest knowledge of or interest in the Sioux way of life. The New York *Times* reviewer, for instance, was impressed with the book's poetic style; and he wrote of Neihardt's account of the Battle of Wounded Knee that, "for such scarifying detail, at once prophetic and horrifying, one will have to go to Tolstoy's 'War and Peace' to find its equal."[10] But this same reviewer did not understand how Neihardt had turned Black Elk's account into a work of literary art, for he spoke of Neihardt as "translator" and praised his "inspired ghost writing." In spite of critical praise, the book did not sell well. The publisher, according to Neihardt, did not realize the book's significance and later remaindered it at forty-five cents a copy.

Black Elk Speaks, however, did not disappear, for it gained a reputation among anthropologists as a valuable primary source book. By some unknown carrier, a copy crossed the Atlantic to Zurich where Carl Jung read and appreciated it as a rich storehouse of Jungian archetypes. Then in 1961 the University of Nebraska Press reissued the book in paperback, and it enjoyed a considerable sale, especially on college campuses. After Neihardt appeared on Dick

Cavett's television show, sales soared; and Pocket Books released an edition of two hundred thousand copies. *Black Elk Speaks* can now be found in almost any bookstore, and the old man's message is, as Neihardt happily declared, "spreading around the world" through translations into eight different languages.

Now required reading in many university courses, it is especially popular on campuses, perhaps because it combines in one volume almost every current preoccupation of students. First, it is a political protest against American imperialism, against manifest destiny, and against the mistreatment of a minority race. *Black Elk Speaks* is also an eloquent plea for conservation and a protest against waste, greed, and conspicuous consumption. A religious book, it is permeated with a mysticism far more genuine and far better suited to this country than the ersatz Hinduism and Buddhism advocated by popular gurus. And the book is also an exciting adventure story, one of the best westerns ever written. In fact, Dee Brown, author of the best-selling Indian history of the American West, *Bury My Heart at Wounded Knee,* calls it the best book on the American Indian; but even Dee Brown did not recognize the fact that *Black Elk Speaks* is not just Black Elk's book but also Neihardt's.[11]

This mistaken notion of the book's true authorship is a common one which Neihardt set straight once and for all during an interview in April, 1971:

Black Elk Speaks is a work of art with two collaborators, the chief one being Black Elk. My function was both creative and editorial. I think he knew the kind of person I was when I came to see him — I am referring to the mystical strain in me and all my work. He said, "You have been sent so that I may teach you and you receive what I know. It was given to me for men and it is true and it is beautiful and soon I will be under the grass." And I think he knew I was the tool — no, the medium — he needed for what he wanted to get said. And my attitude toward what he said to me is one of religious obligation. But it is absurd to suppose that the use of the first person singular is not a literary device, by which I mean that Black Elk did not sit and tell his story in chronological order. At times considerable editing was necessary, but it was always worth the editing. The beginning and the ending are mine; they are what he would have said if he had been able. At times I changed a word, a sentence, sometimes created a paragraph. And the translation — or rather the *transformation* — of what was given me was expressed so that it could be understood by the white world.[12]

Neihardt fleshes the skeleton of Black Elk's memoirs and gives them artistic form. He takes short, choppy sentences and lengthens

them to create a rhythmic flow. He uses every trick of the experienced poet — and Neihardt was by this time a master of literary
devices — to heighten the reader's enjoyment of the narrative. With
his excellent ear for the sound of English words, he exploits every
resource of the language. In *Black Elk Speaks*, one finds alliteration,
assonance, consonance, onomatopoeia, and examples of several
different poetic meters. Some sentences will even scan as if they
were blank verse. More common rhythms, however, are those of the
King James Bible, especially the Book of Psalms. This use of Biblical
rhythms helps to increase the reader's feeling that *Black Elk Speaks*
is a holy book, and makes him realize that Neihardt was absolutely
serious when he said that he had a religious obligation to transmit its
message.

The "holy book" begins like other Neihardt stories, for the old Indian is telling his tale to a white friend. As in both *Indian Tales* and
When the Tree Flowered, this device gives the reader a sense of
returning into the past and a feeling that something extraordinary is
about to be revealed. Black Elk explains the significance of his story
and asserts its universality, for his message "is the story of all life that
is holy and is good to tell, and of us two-leggeds sharing in it with the
four-leggeds and the wings of the air and all green things; for these
are children of one mother and their father is one Spirit."[13] *Black Elk
Speaks*, then, is not simply an entertainment nor a work of social
science expounding upon the amusing customs of a primitive tribe;
instead, it speaks directly to all people because every person is part
of the same whole and comes from the same source of all life. That
source of inspiration and holiness was revealed to Black Elk in his vision, and that revelation makes him a unique person. Though he is
neither a great warrior nor a skilled hunter, he is a prophet; and his
mission is to bring his holy vision to all mankind.

Black Elk Speaks is a tragic book because the old Sioux failed in
his mission, and he admits his failure in the opening chapter in a
lovely passage that Neihardt wrote: "But now that I can see it all as
from a lonely hilltop, I know it was the story of mighty vision given
to a man too weak to use it; of a holy tree that should have flourished
in a people's heart with flowers and singing birds, and now is
withered; and of a people's dream that died in bloody snow." But
redemption comes after the tragedy. In the Christian myth, the
tragedy of Christ's death is followed by redemption and by
everlasting life in Heaven for all believers. Though King Lear dies a
painful death, he discovers the truth at last; and so does Black Elk.

The Sioux have long since been relegated to the reservation where they imitate the worst habits of their conquerors. The buffalo roam mostly in zoos, the sweetwater lakes have silted, but the vision still survives. As Black Elk explains, "But if the vision was true and mighty, as I know, it is true and mighty yet; for such things are of the spirit, and it is in the darkness of their eyes that men get lost."

The function of *Black Elk Speaks* is to preserve this vision so that other men may share it and lift the veil of darkness from their eyes. But, before the old man speaks, he first makes offerings "because no good thing can be done by any man alone." After his prayers to the four quarters of the world, to Wakon Tanka above and to Maka below, he offers the pipe to Neihardt "so that there may be only good between us." Because of these ceremonies, their literary collaboration becomes also a spiritual union. Without this bond, the book would be only reportage, not revelation. Because of it, Neihardt completely absorbs Black Elk's message and becomes his authentic voice.

The problem of finding a proper voice is one of Neihardt's chief concerns. The early lyrics are most successful when Neihardt is surest of his poetic voice. When he is too directly personal, the lyrics become sentimental. In *When the Tree Flowered* and in his best short stories, Neihardt solves the problem of voice and the related technical problem of point of view by using a frame technique in which a young white man asks an old Indian to tell a story, which is exactly what he does in *Black Elk Speaks*. Though Neihardt says that Black Elk spoke through him, it is equally correct to say that Neihardt speaks through Black Elk, since the Sioux holy man asserts many of Neihardt's personal beliefs and dramatizes in his narrative some of Neihardt's favorite themes.

The first such theme is greed. Black Elk's earliest memories are of white men, the Wasichus, thronging to the Black Hills in search of gold, "the yellow metal that they worship and that makes them crazy"; and many characters in Neihardt's early novel, *Life's Lure*, are destroyed by this same insanity. At first, the white men seem calm and reasonable; they only want a little land to make a road. But, as their madness grows, they begin to destroy the harmony of Sioux life by demanding more and more. Black Elk describes the downfall of his people in one short paragraph which also summarizes the entire history of the westward movement from the Indian point of view: "Once we were happy in our own country and we were seldom hungry, for then the two-leggeds and the four-leggeds lived together like relatives, and there was plenty for them and for us. But the Wasichus came, and they have made little islands for us and other little islands for the four-legged, and always these islands are becoming smaller, for around them surges the gnawing flood of the Wasichu; and it is dirty with lies and greed."

When the harmonious relationship between man and nature is violated by greedy men, nature retaliates; but, since her blind justice punishes the innocent along with the guilty, Black Elk remembers a hungry winter. But the hungry winter is followed by a happy summer when the Wasichus promise to go away for as long as grass grows and water flows. As a result, the Sioux can hope and dream again. In contrast to the Wasichus, who live only for gain, the Sioux are satisfied with what they have. Though they may want more ponies or better guns, they desire little else. For example, a gift of warm slippers makes Eagle Voice a happy man in *When the Tree Flowered*. Because the Sioux are less encumbered by possessions than the Wasichus, they can dream dreams and see visions.

The greatest of many such visions in Neihardt's Indian stories is described in the third chapter of *Black Elk Speaks*, which contains some of the most remarkable passages in contemporary literature. Considered solely as a literary *tour-de-force*, it is astounding; but it is more than just a spectacular performance because it is completely authentic and achieves the level of myth, prophecy, or revelation. Black Elk's vision is as forceful and as convincing as any thing in the Bible because Neihardt makes one believe in it. By this point in the narrative, the reader trusts Black Elk because his voice is genuine.

Black Elk receives this vision in 1871, when he is only nine years old. At first he hears a voice calling him, just as he heard a similar voice four years earlier. This time, however, his legs, arms, and face swell; and two spirits come from the clouds and transport him to a snowy plain. In paraphrase, this incident may sound like mumbo-jumbo; but, in Neihardt's poetic prose, the reader shares the experience with Black Elk. The reader's imagination is engaged by a series of striking images which remove him from the ordinary. The first two chapters of *Black Elk Speaks* utilize only the faculty of rational understanding, but these images in the third chapter cause the reader to transcend the rational and enter the realm of spirit. Like a Transcendentalist, Neihardt works through nature to spirit, from the ordinary to the visionary:

> I looked and saw a bay horse standing there, and he began to speak: "Behold me!" he said, "my life-history you shall see." Then he wheeled

about to where the sun goes down, and said: "Behold them! Their history
you shall know."

I looked, and there were twelve black horses yonder all abreast with
necklaces of bison hoofs, and they were beautiful, but I was frightened,
because their manes were lightning, and there was thunder in their nostrils.

Then the bay horse wheeled to where the great white giant lives (the
north) and said: "Behold!" And yonder there were twelve white horses all
abreast. Their manes were flowing like a blizzard wind and from their noses
came a roaring, and all about them white geese soared and circled.

As the vision continues through each of the four directions, young
Black Elk is presented with the Sioux cosmology described in *When
the Tree Flowered*; but he has a more significant experience. The Six
Grandfathers, who represent the six powers of the world (the four
cardinal directions plus the earth and the sky) speak to him of his
people's destiny, and each Grandfather presents him with a symbolic
gift. Black Elk then rides the bay horse across a wonderful prairie to
the very heart of the sacred hoop, and there he has a vision of the
good life which is both simple and profound — simple and direct in
its language; profound in the connotations of its words. He takes a
bright red stick, one of the gifts given to him by the Grandfathers,
and thrusts it into the earth: "As it touched the earth it leaped
mightily in my hand and was a waga chun, the rustling tree, very tall
and full of leafy branches and of all birds singing. And beneath it all
the animals were mingling with the people like relatives and making
happy cries. The women raised their tremolo of joy, and the men
shouted all together: 'Here we shall raise our children and be as little
chickens under the mother sheo's wing.' "

From this joyful revelation, Black Elk is carried onward to see a
darker place. The old man, who was illiterate and knew nothing of
the world outside Pine Ridge, remarked to Neihardt, "I think we are
near that place now, and I am afraid something very bad is going to
happen all over the world." In 1931, the world was very much like
Black Elk's description of what he saw in his vision: "Then the people broke camp again, and saw the black road before them towards
where the sun goes down, and black clouds coming yonder; and they
did not want to go but could not stay. And as they walked the third
ascent, all the animals and fowls that were the people ran here and
there, for each one seemed to have his own little vision that he
followed and his own rules; and all over the universe I could hear the
winds at war like wild beasts fighting."

This lack of a unified vision of the good life is what causes most of

man's problems, according to several other works by Neihardt.
When men think only in terms of themselves, they destroy both
themselves and the people around them through the sin of *hubris*,
which also dooms the heroes of classical tragedy. The Sioux warrior
is proud, but for his people and not for himself. Doing brave deeds
and making kill-talks is fine only if a warrior does not forget to thank
the gods. A hunter gains status within the tribe when he gives his kill
to those who are less fortunate. In poem after poem and in story after
story, Neihardt shows that the inevitable result of selfishness is
death. The ideal is total selflessness, the third stage in the process of
discovering Nirvana. "The Red Wind," in Neihardt's early lyric by
that title, blows over countries whose rulers have been selfish.

In his vision, Black Elk sees, therefore, both an ideal existence and
its opposite in brilliant metaphors which work directly on the
reader's imagination and make him see them through Black Elk's
eyes. When the boy returns to consciousness after twelve days, his
parents tell him that he has been sick; in fact, he has been thought
dead — and he has been almost like young John Neihardt was when
he had a similar vision at about the same age. Old Black Elk
remembers that he could not understand his vision but that he could
always recall the pictures. From this time on, he is a special person
who devotes the rest of his life to realizing his ideal vision of the
proper way to live.

In succeeding chapters, Black Elk describes a bison hunt, the
courting of his friend High Horse, and several battles with the
Wasichus that lead up the destruction of "Long Hair" that is,
Custer on the Greasy Grass. These stories closely resemble those in
When the Tree Flowered, which come from the same source; but
they are lively, colorful, authentic, and often exciting. In these
episodes, Black Elk does not seem much different from any other
young Sioux. After the Battle of Little Big Horn, for example, he cuts
off the finger joint of a dead soldier — not a particularly noble action
but one fully in keeping with his character. After the victory over
Custer, however, bad times begin as the Sioux walk the black road of
pain and suffering because they dared oppose Wasichu greed.

In these chapters of *Black Elk Speaks*, the narrative is particularly
moving. Indeed, these chapters, which are prose versions of the excellent *Song of the Indian Wars* and *Song of the Messiah* from *A Cycle of the West*, show how the magnificent vision slowly dis-
integrates as the Sioux tribe wanders in the wilderness. Like an Old
Testament prophet seeking a way to rescue the Children of Israel

and redeem them in God's eyes, Black Elk searches for another revelation. However, the death of Crazy Horse in 1877 is a special blow to him because Crazy Horse seemed to embody the spirit of the Lakota (which is what the Sioux call themselves), much like a Joshua or a David. Black Elk is still only a boy, but he wants to be the same kind of leader. Finding temporary refuge in Grandmother's Land (Canada), he wonders if his power will grow so that he may "make the holy tree to flower in the center and find the red road again." But he thinks that his people would say, "What can you do if even Sitting Bull can do nothing?"

Later on, however, Black Elk dances the Horse Dance; and, while he sings a sacred song, his vision returns and gives him new hope for the future. From that day on, he always rises early to see the daybreak star of understanding; and his people begin to realize his gift. But understanding is not enough, and the reader shares Black Elk's growing frustration: he is not a whole person because he cannot unite thought with action. He uses his power to heal the sick, but he cannot heal an ailing nation: "If a man or woman or child dies, it does not matter long, for the nation lives on. It was the nation that was dying, and the vision was for the nation; but I have done nothing with it."

The reader grieves with Black Elk as the bison dwindle, and he feels his sorrow at the criminal waste left by railroad hunters who killed the bison for only a slice of hump. To get new ideas about how to make the sacred tree bloom once more, Black Elk joins Buffalo Bill's Wild West Show and travels across the Atlantic. He gets to meet Grandmother England (Queen Victoria), who tells him that, if the Lakota were her people, she would treat them better; but he learns nothing that will help his people.

When Black Elk returns to America, he finds his people converted to the Ghost Dance religion, the last futile gesture by the Plains Indians to restore the old way (discussed in detail in Chapter 5). His reaction is similar to that of Eagle Voice in *When the Tree Flowered*, which is not surprising since that novel is based partly on Black Elk's memories. In fact, Black Elk's own vision becomes all the more convincing in this chapter since he compares it to the false vision of Wovoka; but, because Black Elk also wants to believe Wovoka, he performs the Ghost Dance, which is supposed to allow the dancer to visit the spirit world and to talk to his dead relatives, who would, according to Wovoka, eventually come back to earth again, along with the buffalo, while the Wasichu would vanish forever. But Black Elk is disappointed; for, when he awakens from his vision, the flowering tree is dead.

This loss of unity and vitality which characterizes the death of Lakota culture is the final tragedy of *Black Elk Speaks*. The cavalry sees the Ghost Dance as a threat, and it mounts one last bloody campaign. As Black Elk watches the butchering of women and children at Wounded Knee in 1890, he knows that his great dream has ended. Yet, the reader is left with some consolation: the power of Black Elk's vision is still present in his book and in the example of his life. Neihardt demonstrates this power in a postscript by explaining how he arranged for the old man to take a trip to Harney Peak in the Black Hills, the spot where he first received his vision. On the way, Black Elk remarks, "If I have any power left, the thunder beings of the west should hear me when I send a voice, and there should at least be a little thunder and a little rain."

On a cloudless day, in a season of drought, the old man begins a prayer to the Great Spirit. " 'Again, and maybe for the last time on this earth, I recall the great vision you sent me. It may be that some little root of the sacred tree still lives. Nourish it then, that it may leaf and bloom and fill with singing birds. Hear me, not for myself, but for my people; I am old. Hear me that they may once more go back into the sacred hoop and find the good red road, the shielding tree!' " This prayer is Black Elk's affirmation of faith in his vision of what life should be, an affirmation made in spite of his personal tragedy and the tragedy of his nation.

As the old man stands on the mountaintop, rain begins to fall upon his aged face.

CHAPTER 5

Epic Poetry

I The Divine Enchantment

NEIHARDT'S first published attempt at epic poetry, *The Divine Enchantment*, presents Hindu mythology in turgid blank verse and, as the poet himself once said, constitutes "the case of posterity against John G. Neihardt." Though Neihardt later burned every copy he could find, the poem is a promising work. That Neihardt, then a poor teenager who worked in the potato fields, could conceive such a work, let alone write it, is actually quite remarkable. Moreover, this poem demonstrates his determination to become not simply an ordinary poet but a visionary bard. At the time he composed *The Divine Enchantment*, his poetic ability was, of course, not equal to such a grand project; but, if the poem lacks both polish and genius, it does show considerable talent.

The story chosen by the "outsetting bard" is taken from his avid reading of the *Upanishads, The Vedanta Philosophy* by Max Muller, and *The Bible in India* by Louis Jacolliot.[1] It is a Hindu myth with Christian parallels, and Neihardt considerably provides a prose summary at the beginning of the little book which was published at his expense. In the story, the maiden Devanaguy is destined to bear Christna, the incarnation of Vishnu; but a jealous and fearful tyrant, Kansa, has her imprisoned. During her imprisonment, however, Vishnu appears and "overshadows" her. As Neihardt explains, "During the term of her gestation, Devanaguy was transported by a continual, ecstatic dream. Her spirit, freed from her body, ran through every pulse of passion, felt the dark terrors of the Void, and wantoned in the unwinged blue: thus giving to the unborn child, inherently, that for which the sages vainly sought."[2]

To dramatize such a vague dream would tax the ability of a mature artist, much less that of a sixteen-year-old boy. To succeed would require the wisdom of a sage and the imagination of a prophet. But, with a confidence born of youth, ignorance, and zeal fired by his constant reading, Neihardt plunged ahead. At this period of his life, he must have resembled Fitzgerald's young James Gatz when, on the verge of turning himself into The Great Gatsby, "his heart was in a constant, turbulent riot." Like the hero of Fitzgerald's novel, Neihardt had reveries which may have been "a satisfactory hint of the unreality of reality, a promise that the rock of the world was founded securely on a fairy's wing."[3]

Young Neihardt's enormous literary energy and his insatiable appetite for words are evident throughout the poem. In spite of its many faults, *The Divine Enchantment* is full of high spirits — so full, in fact, that the poem soars into the empyrean without the necessary metaphorical ties to earth. Instead of embodying its abstract ideas in concrete symbols, it features dark abysses, immortal blisses, and "long ecstatic bursts of melody." Yet one cannot help liking an earnest young man so full of literature that he could write this passionate apostrophe to evening which begins the poem:

> O Evening, dusky daughter of the Day,
> Multiloquent in silence, passioned, calm;
> Thou seemest to me a lovely Yadu maid,
> Whose cheek though browned, yet blushes with the pulse
> Of love and summer; while a languid soul
> Dreams in the dark, deep eyes, that placid, hint
> Of all the tropic passion they can flash
> When love has charmed them or when hate has stirred.[4]

Lush, unrestrained, sentimental — this passage commits all these literary sins and more; but too much enthusiasm is better than too little. As critic Randolph Bourne, one of Neihardt's contemporaries, put it, "Prudence is a dreadful thing in youth."

After chanting "Om," the magic syllable, Devanaguy, the virgin heroine of *The Divine Enchantment*, finds peaceful sleep and begins the dream which continues throughout the poem and which climaxes in her achievement of Nirvana. In dreaming, she finds release from ordinary mortal life and discovers the spiritual truth of self-forgetfulness; however, her dream is much too vague for the reader to understand its spiritual significance, at least not without a considerable knowledge of Hinduism. Moreover, the reader cannot develop any sympathy for the characters who are not of flesh-and-blood but ethereal abstractions. Because of these obvious faults, therefore, *The Divine Enchantment* is of interest only because it is Neihardt's first published attempt at epic poetry.

One critic views this poem as a preliminary version of the philosophy of spiritual awareness which Neihardt articulated twenty-five years later in *Poetic Values*.[5] In that book, Neihardt speaks of the meaning of Nirvana, which can only be achieved when one realizes that the individual self is unimportant. By comparing *The Divine Enchantment* with his later work, one can see his strong, consistent development from a boy who loved words and had big dreams to a mature poet who found ways to realize his ideals and to communicate them to a large audience of readers.

II   A Cycle of the West

Neihardt's epic dreams were finally realized in 1949 with the publication in one volume of his five epic songs — *The Song of Three Friends, The Song of Hugh Glass, The Song of Jed Smith, The Song of the Indian Wars,* and *The Song of the Messiah* — which fill more than six hundred and fifty pages and contain more than sixteen thousand lines in heroic couplets. Neihardt spent almost thirty years, more than five thousand days, writing *A Cycle of the West*, and the result was a poem as long as the *Illiad* and the *Odyssey*, more than twice as long as Steven Vincent Benét's *John Brown's Body*, and three times the length of Archibald MacLeish's *Conquistador*, to name two other modern American epics. It is, in fact, probably the longest poem ever written by an American.

Mere size is, of course, no guarantee of quality; but *A Cycle of the West* is more than six hundred and fifty pages of *good* blank verse, of often excellent blank verse. It is not a collection of five separate long poems, as it might seem at first, but a unified work built around one central theme which runs throughout the entire narrative: the conquest of the Missouri River Valley from 1822 to 1890. Because of its high quality, it deserves the title of America's national epic more than any other poem, with the possible exception of Whitman's "Song of Myself," a greater poem but one which does not fit the usual definitions of epic poetry. For the first time in the entire literary history of the United States, the "matter of America" has found a chronicler worthy of it. In *The River and I, The Splendid Wayfaring*, and other books, Neihardt asserts that the settlement of the West is a theme every bit as heroic as the fall of either Troy or Adam. He was, he often asserts, "more thrilled by the history of the Lewis and Clark expedition than by the tale of Jason," and he shares in *A Cycle of the West* such thrills with his readers. In this poem, Neihardt defies the genteel tradition, which went to Europe for its literary models and inspiration, and the narrow, limited New

Humanism, which criticized uncouth writers who expressed the big truths of this country. Instead, Neihardt's motive is the same as Walt Whitman's — to give a full, poetic exression of America's hearty, energetic spirit.

The search for an American epic is as old as American literature itself. In 1785, Timothy Dwight published *The Conquest of Canaan*, an epic poem in heroic couplets about Joshua's passage into Israel. Its readers, according to one noted critic, "had little trouble convincing themselves that Joshua was Washington, and that other American heroes strode thinly disguised through its eleven tedious books."[6] Joel Barlow published an American epic while still a student at Yale, his *The Vision of Columbus* (1785), in which he tries to cover all of American history in nine books and which contains long rhapsodic passages about America's bright future. But, besides these early attempts, few Americans found their new country a fit subject for epic verse. In *The Octopus* (1900), one of Frank Norris's leading characters is a young poet named Presley who wants to write an epic of the West, using "some vast tremendous theme, heroic, terrible, to be unrolled in all the thundering progression of hexameters,"[7] but Presley fails to realize his ambition. In another essay, "A Neglected Epic," Norris anticipates Neihardt's theories of epic poetry.[8] Like Neihardt, he saw the westward movement as one of the crucial events in all history; for it led the western people on their final step back to "the vague and mysterious East."

Walt Whitman, thirty years before Norris, had used the completion of Cyrus Field's Atlantic cable and the building of the Suez Canal to symbolize the same journey from the West to the East in his famous poem "Passage to India." For Whitman the westward movement was more than just a simple search for land and wealth: it represented a fulfillment of the vision of Columbus, the same vision that Joel Barlow had dreamed about. Whitman, like other Transcendentalists, was interested in Eastern philosophy. The final leg of the westward journey would, he believed, provide Western man with a chance to realize the ideal by combining Western ingenuity with Eastern wisdom. Like Whitman, Neihardt was also fascinated by Oriental Mysticism, as *The Divine Enchantment* demonstrates. Although he did not complete a "passage to India" in *A Cycle of the West*, he found in the Sioux religion an American equivalent of Hinduism, for the American Indian also had his origins in the East.

Although *A Cycle of the West* comes closer than any other poem to being a national epic, it is little read today and seldom rates mention in the literary histories. Perhaps one reason for this critical neglect is that the poem is determinedly old-fashioned because Neihardt wished to appeal to a wide audience. In fact, Neihardt sometimes overuses such poetic archaisms as " 'twas" and "alas." Lucy Lockwood Hazard, in *The Frontier in American Literature*, complains about Neihardt's classical allusions, his "painfully elaborate figures of speech," his excessive description, and his authorical intrusions into the narrative.[9] These criticisms are justified. Since *A Cycle* contains more than sixteen thousand lines, it is easy enough to leaf through and find a few bad lines, a few soporific passages.

But, since even Homer nodded, the critic should not tax Neihardt too much for occasional lapses; instead, the poem should be judged according to its total worth; and, if judged on that basis, it is a major achievement. As one critic wisely points out, "But against the record of excess, of flawed language, undeniably there, must be balanced a transcendent achievement, an ultimate impact, of several hundred pages devoted to a love affair with a region."[10] The same critic recognizes that "*Cycle* is a step toward that elusive identity, a long American poem which celebrates the timeless themes of Creation, Warfare, Journey, and Settlement intensely, urgently, and transcendentally in a prosody that endows the American language with dignity and sobriety."

Neihardt had an excellent reason for the literary techniques he uses in the poem, a reason that is easy to understand when one has read the prose works that serve as background. Neihardt wanted to assert the universal significance of his material and to assert also his kinship with Homer, Virgil, and Milton. Neihardt is always conscious, sometimes perhaps too conscious, that he is writing in the epic tradition. Another reason for choosing a conventional form was his desire to reach a larger audience than most contemporary poets hope for. One of Neihardt's goals in writing the poem was to make Americans aware of their heritage, to make them realize that the westward movement involved more than cowboys and covered wagons; and he succeeded so well that the first two songs in *A Cycle* were reprinted for the schoolchildren of Nebraska. He made Nebraskans feel proud of themselves and their land, which is why the legislature made him the state's poet laureate. Also, by the time Neihardt began work on the poem, he had abandoned his various experiments with poetic form: he had learned that the discipline imposed by blank verse was good for his art.

Neihardt's use of the heroic couplet does not mean that *A Cycle of*

the West is rigidly or monotonously formal, for its author was a
master of metrics who knew how to vary his lines by shifting the
caesural pause and by alternating run-on and end-stopped couplets.
He also desired to tell a good story, and the poem is often as swift
moving and exciting as a good western film. Neihardt alternates action scenes with his reflections upon them so that the reader never
gets the impression that he is moralizing too much, a tendency
which mars the quality of his early novels and poems. For this
reason, *A Cycle* can be read profitably by both Nebraska schoolchildren and sophisticated literary critics. Like the best books in any
genre or in any language, it speaks to everyone.

III   The Song of Three Friends

A Cycle of the West begins with *The Song of Three Friends*, the
second of the five songs to be completed; and it relates the story of
Mike Fink, Will Carpenter, and Frank Talbeau. Mike Fink was a
real person, a keelboatman who traveled up the Missouri with the
Ashley-Henry men and died a mysterious death after a quarrel; but
Mike Fink is also an American folk hero who is a half-horse, a half-
alligator of superhuman strength who ranks just below Davy
Crockett; in fact, some stories have Fink winning a shooting match
between the two. Neihardt told Fink's story briefly in the *The Splendid Warfaring*, and he tries in this poem to discover Fink's full
significance.

The Song of Three Friends begins with a paean to Ashley's Hundred, a band of fur trappers that, to Neihardt, seems an epic company. Although their time is long over, their memory will live
forever, for they have become "comrades of Jason and his crew."
The fleece they seek belongs not to a golden ram but to a beaver, but
they are no less relentless in their search than the Argonauts. As
Neihardt does throughout *A Cycle*, he uses classical allusions not as a
means of displaying his erudition, which was considerable, but as a
way of drawing parallels between past and present. The voyage of
Ashley's canoes is, therefore, comparable to the last stage of a voyage
begun by Greek galleys.

As the voyageurs laugh and joke in camp, Neihardt introduces his
three main characters, one strong, English Saxon, one Norman Vi-
king, and one small, clever Celt; but it is more likely that Saxon
Mike Fink was actually of Pennsylvania German stock. By using
each man as a representative of his ethnic group, Neihardt is trying
to emphasize the international, "Aryan" Westward Movement.

Carpenter, the first to be introduced, is six feet and two inches tall and weighs two hundred pounds, a big man for a big country. A handsome Norman blond, Carpenter contrasts with Fink's dark Saxon complexion; and he is as silent as Fink is noisy. Historians know little about the actual Carpenter but enough about the real Mike Fink to know that Neihardt makes some major changes in his character. In most of the folklore stories, Mike Fink is a rough brawler who once shot off a slave's protruding heel because the sight offended him. Neihardt's Fink is an equally good fighter, but he is much more heroic; and this change is perhaps the most serious flaw in *The Song of Three Friends*, since a more realistic Fink would have added both authenticity and interest. Neihardt's description of him is too elevated, too literary:

> The Rabelaisian stories of the rogue
> Ran wedded to the richness of his brogue.
> And wheresoever boatmen came to drink,
> There someone broached some escapade of Fink
> That might well fill the goat-hoofed with delight;
> For Mike, the pantagruelizing wight
> Was happy in the health of bone and braun
> And had the code and conscience of the faun
> To guide him blithely down the easy way.[11]

Although "Rabelaisian" is suggestive, "pantagruelizing wight" hardly seems too much a "literary" phrase to apply to a "ring-tailed roarer," as the boisterous keelboatman is called in the folklore stories. Neihardt describes Fink this way because he knows that the boatman is "a questionable hero," and he wants to concentrate on the heroic struggle of these men, not on their baser appetites. Fink's body, for instance, has the shape of "God's Adamic dream."

Like many other American writers, Neihardt uses the theme of the American Adam, a new man for a new world.[12] He wants to show the fur trapper as a special type, as a man larger than life. His trappers, much like the cowboys of popular literature, are strong men who live by a code of personal honor much like that of medieval knights. This concept makes Neihardt's heroic songs seem more like Tennyson's *Idylls of the King*, one of Neihardt's boyhood favorites; but he has to distort history in order to treat Mike Fink in this fashion. For this reason, *The Song of Three Friends* suffers from comparison to the more authentic poems in *A Cycle*. This flaw, however, does not seem major after the narrative gets underway. Fink, Carpenter, and little

Frank Talbeau, a genial Frenchman, are the best of friends who fight together in the wilderness; and, after Neihardt stops generalizing and has them on the mighty Missouri, the poem begins to develop rapidly.

Neihardt, at his best in describing the scene around them, uses his heroic epithets that seem most appropriate; for the country is vast, strong, and almost infinite in its long prairie that sweeps to the horizon. Neihardt knew this country well; for, as he proudly explains in his preface to *A Cycle*, "If I write of hot-winds and grasshoppers, of prairie fires and blizzards, of dawns and noons and sunsets and nights of brooding heat and thunderstorms and vast lands, I knew them early." In this passage, for example, Fink's party arrives at its wintering place, an Indian village along the Musselshell River:

> A strip of poplars stretched
> Along a winding stream, their bare boughs etched
> Black line by line upon a flat of snow
> Blue tinted in the falling afterglow.
> Humped ponies 'mid the drifts and clumps of sage
> Went nosing after grudging pasturage
> Where'er it chanced the blizzards' whimsic flaws
> Had swept the slough grass bare. A flock of squaws
> Chopped wood and chattered in the underbrush,
> Their ax strokes thudding dully in the hush.
> Their nasal voices rising shrill and clear.

These lines have beauty, action, character, and force. The strip of poplars outlined black against the snow is a painterly description that makes the reader see. The flock of squaws chatter like birds in the crisp air, and the reader can hear the strokes of their axes. Neihardt's verbs are strong and forceful. Despite the archaic "Where'er," the passage is fresh, lively, and true.

Neihardt also uses the descriptions of natural scenes to make moral comments without moralizing. He reads nature like the Romantic poet that he is. Before Fink's men arrive at the Musselshell, for instance, they must pass through a landscape that corresponds to the men's own loneliness; and they are confronted with "a vast serenity of death." In *The River and I*, Neihardt writes about how a single coyote affected him; in *The Song of Three Friends*, he also dramatizes the terrible dry loneliness of the place with a single "loping kiote." Neihardt's trappers belong to this hostile land, and their personalities are shaped by it. Throughout *A Cycle*, the identification of character with setting is masterful.

Because the reader sees the land so clearly, the men who try to conquer it are also presented to him.

Meanwhile, when back on the Musselshell, Fink, Talbeau, and Carpenter dally in the camp of the Bloods, where the chief's half-breed daughter attracts both Fink and Carpenter. This prairie Helen hesitates, then chooses, in a passage which ends the fourth section of the poem with a proper climax; for Neihardt knows well how to build suspense:

> She stops before another tent and stoops,
> Her fingers feeling for the buckskin loops
> That bind the rawhide flaps. 'Tis opened wide,
> The slant white light of morning falls inside,
> And half the town may witness at whose feet
> She sets the little pot of steaming meat —
> 'Tis Carpenter.

Talbeau tries to mediate the ensuing quarrel over the chief's daughter between his two old friends but fails; and when Fink sinks into melancholy as the winter deepens, nature is again a clue to a character's mood. When Fink and Carpenter finally fight, Neihardt's description of their battle shows that he could write a good action scene as well as descriptive verse. The poetry matches the swift and violent battle because the sentences are shorter in order to make the lines move faster. Neihardt uses onomatopoeia in such phrases as "thud of knuckles" to recreate the sound of a noisy brawl. The imagery about such fierce animals as dogs, bulls, and bears matches the animalistic struggle of Fink and Carpenter. Since two savage males are fighting over a mate, the trappers are stripped of any literary pretensions; for their struggle reflects only their basic drives. Their old spirit of comradeship, about which Talbeau keeps reminding them, is forgotten because passion is stronger than honor, more important than good will.

In Neihardt's stories about mountain men, this change often occurs. Two comrades, men who have always respected one another, are suddenly confronted with a basic, natural force which drives them apart. In *Song of Three Friends*, that force is love, or rather lust, since neither Fink nor Carpenter seems especially tender in his feelings for the girl. The same theme occurs in the short stories "The Scars" and "The Red Roan Mare"; in another story, "The Deuces," a prairie fire drives one man to desert his friend; in *The Song of Hugh Glass*, the threat of Indian attack does so. In each case, one of the comrades forgets the lessons of noble philosophy; and, in each instance, he is finally punished for not honoring his obligation to his fellow man. Neihardt believes that man can survive in a hostile country only if he is true to the best in himself. If he tries to live like a beast, he will certainly die like one.

By stripping away man's pretensions and by removing him from his philosophy, religion, and morality, Neihardt reveals what men are like without the heroic selflessness constantly advocated in his many books. When man becomes interested solely in a material goal — a fine squaw, a mining claim as in *Life's Lure*, or a thick pack of beaver pelts — he loses everything which makes life worthwhile. In *A Cycle of the West*, Neihardt presents examples of men who have proper attitudes toward life such as Jed Smith and Chief Crazy Horse; and he contrasts them to those who are the real savages. In this way, Neihardt's descriptions of character fit his ethical philosophy, as does the action of the poem. When a man fights only for himself, he turns himself into a beast. Selfishness dooms fur trappers just as it does the famous tragic heroes.

And such is the fate of Mike Fink. After the brawl, Talbeau again tries to make peace by asking Mike to perform his old trick — shoot a tin cup off Carpenter's head. This time, however, Fink misses; and, though he swears he did not mean to do it, Fink, the American Adam, is branded with the mark of Cain. Having sinned, he must be punished; and his nemesis is little Frank Talbeau. Thus begins a long chase which closely resembles the crawl of Hugh Glass which Neihardt describes in the second song of *A Cycle*. Talbeau catches the sleeping Fink, steals his gun and water flasks, and then orders him to walk east across a rocky desert: "That region of despair/ Should be Mike's purgatory!" Neihardt's gift for description is especially evident, for the desert is a perfect metaphor for the spiritual bleakness of Mike Fink; and, as Fink trudges on, nature becomes his torturer:

> He came to where converging gulches made
> A steep-walled basin for the blinding glare.
> Here, fanged and famished, crawled the prickly pear;
> Malevolent with thirst, the soap weed thrust
> Its barbed stilletos from the arid dust,
> Defiant of the rain-withholding blue:
> And in the midst a lonely scrub oak grew,
> A crooked dwarf, that in the pictured bog
> Of its own shadow, squatted like a frog.

As Fink stumbles through this terrible punishment with Talbeau always at his heels, he cannot find a moment's peace. Neihardt demonstrates how even the strongest, most heroic man may destroy himself, for it is not really Talbeau who punishes Fink. Little Frank is only the agency of some higher power or greater force, unnamed and vague, but always present. Fink, who realizes this fact, begs for forgiveness, for consolation, for just one drop of water; but, since Western justice is not merciful, Talbeau cannot forgive him.

Like Hugh Glass, in the second song of *A Cycle*, Talbeau wants his vengeance; but he begins to think about the ethical consequences of his own action. By driving Fink, is he not himself becoming inhumane? But by the time he decides to forgive Mike, it is too late; when he finds Fink, the boatman is already dead. The tragedy is now doubled: Fink and Talbeau are both denied redemption because each refused to honor his fellow man. Both sought vengeance, and vengeance is self-defeating. *The Song of Three Friends* ends on a note of horror. As Talbeau trudges across the desert in hopes of finding his friend, he spies a flock of crows, which guides him to the eyeless corpse of his former comrade. Thus, "the jeering chorus of the crows" is all that remains for Frank Talbeau. Three men, all fine, noble, Adamic heroes, have dwindled to one sad, little man because of the selfishness of two, and because the other one refused to obey the commandment, "Vengeance is mine." *The Song of Three Friends* is a powerful indictment of man's self-centered refusal to live up to his own best possibilities.

Almost all first reviewers of this epic were impressed by its power and force, although a few found it less enthralling than *The Song of Hugh Glass*.[13] As the Boston *Transcript* critic observed, "There are numerous fine descriptive passages, and the action goes forward with vigorous sweeps. Time and time again one falls upon exquisitely beautiful lines that fasten a landscape or make a mood thrilling."[14] Though *The Song of Three Friends* was highly praised and was later reprinted in a school edition, it is, unfortunately, little read today.

IV   The Song of Hugh Glass

The second book of the complete edition of *A Cycle of the West* is *The Song of Hugh Glass*; and, as the first of Neihardt's epic songs to be published, it was highly praised as something new in American literature. This passage from the *Yale Review* is typical of the praise heaped upon the poem from almost every critic: "Nothing can define the nature of this book but a reading of it — and that is an experience worth living indeed. It is to have caught up for you into a work that is to belong to world literature, the places you have seen, where you may have lived or where your friends may live; the deeds of brave men which are your heritage and which are more integral to your past than ever the events of the Aeneid were to the Romans or those of the Arthuriad to the Britons."[15]

In *The Song of Hugh Glass*, which is another true story of the Ashley-Henry men, Hugh Glass, an old trapper who still retains titanic strength, is dispatched as an advance man to find a campsite and to kill fresh meat for the main body of trappers. When they catch up with him, they discover that he has been horribly mauled by a grizzly and that his death seems inevitable. Leaving him in the care of his best friend, a handsome youth named Jamie, and another trapper, Jules LeBon, the main party forges ahead. While Jamie and Jules wait with him, Glass grows steadily weaker but refuses to die. When it appears that the three of them will soon be attacked by a Ree war party, Jules persuades Jamie to leave his old friend, who is still unconscious, and flee.

But the Indians overlook Hugh, and he does not die. Instead, he regains consciousness; and, filled with a lust for vengeance against his former comrades, he crawls one hundred miles to get help. After his near-miraculous recovery, he pursues Jamie; but, when they finally meet, old Hugh forgives the boy. This story had particular appeal for Neihardt, and he explains why in *The Splendid Wayfaring*: "If, when the long pursuit was ended, Hugh had wrought vengeance upon his youthful betrayer, his adventure would have been nothing more than an astounding feat of endurance and ferocity; but in the end the Graybeard forgave, and that fact raises his story to the level of sublimity."[16]

The poem begins with the friendship between Glass and Jamie, Graybeard and Goldhair as Neihardt calls them. The old man is a sort of Captain Ahab because some deep hatred eats him "like a still, white hell." "Gray-bearded, gray of eye and crowned with gray," he is like some old tragic king, a Lear or an Agamemnon. Yet Hugh, like Ahab, has his humanity; and his sympathies are awakened by young Jamie, who is both son and innocent lover for the old man. Although *The Song of Hugh Glass* contains no overt homosexuality, the relationship between Jamie and Hugh has many parallels in classic American literature. In the wilderness, the sidekick replaces the hero's wife and offers another kind of love. Huck and Jim in Mark Twain's *Huckleberry Finn*, Ishmael and Queequeg in Herman Melville's *Moby Dick*, Natty Bumppo and Chingachgook in James Fenimore Cooper's *Leatherstocking Tales* all prefer each other's company to that of women. Without his friend, the hero is lost; and this relationship exists between Hugh and Jamie. In an excellent passage of narrative verse, Neihardt describes how the power of love moved the old man to desperate action when, involved in a fight with the savage Rees, Jamie foolishly refuses to retreat:

> 'Twas then old Hugh
> Tore off the gray mask, and the heart shone through.
> For, halting in a dry, flood-guttered draw,
> The trappers rallied, looked aloft and saw
> That travesty of war against the sky.
> Out of breathless hush, the old man's cry
> Leaped shivering, an anguished cry and wild
> As of some mother fearing for her child,
> And up the steep he went with mighty bounds,
> Long afterward the story went the rounds,
> How old Glass fought that day. With gun for club,
> Grim as a grizzly fighting for a cub,
> He laid about him, cleared the way, and so,
> Supported by the firing from below,
> Brought Jamie back.

In the classic American novels, the hero's friend is of another race and possesses contrasting "gifts," as Cooper calls them. Queequeg carries his god about with him in a leather pouch and Jim has his famous hair ball. In *The Song of Hugh Glass*, the contrast is not one of race or religion but one of age and also of the difference between innocence and experience. The friendship of Hugh and Jamie closely resembles the friendship between Saul and David. Hugh is the old king, once mighty but now near death; and Jamie is the beautiful boy who entertains him and brings joy into his life.

When Jamie discovers Hugh's mangled body after the grizzly's attack, the tragedy of betrayal begins. Hugh wrestles with death, and nature seems to sympathize, as it often does in *A Cycle of the West*. Man, Neihardt believes, is noble chiefly because he will not yield without a fight. The other trappers lack Hugh's nobility because they cannot understand the true meaning of his struggle against death; instead, they speculate about how long a mangled man can

last and even make bets. When they leave Jules and Jamie alone
with the old man, Jules becomes Neihardt's representative of the
reasonable man; for, like most ordinary people, he wants to
rationalize Hugh's inevitable death. In truth, of course, Jules is
afraid of being left alone in hostile country and is staying only
because of the extra money offered him. He is a weak person, but he
thinks like a normal man with normal fears: staying with Hugh is
just not sensible. Here, and throughout *The Song of Hugh Glass*,
Neihardt contrasts the ordinary man with the extraordinary epic
hero. Jules is not an Iago, but the evil that he does is just as great.
Neihardt believes that men must transcend their ordinary mortal
weaknesses or their reasonable, sensible arguments drag them to
Hell.

Jamie is torn between two choices: he can behave like an ordinary
man and follow Jules LeBon's advice, the sensible reasoning of Jules
the Good; or he can stay with his friend. Although Jamie knows that
the Rees may attack at any moment and although he wonders why
he should die for a hopeless cause, his friendship with Hugh
transcends his knowledge because love is an immortal force.
Neihardt's description of Jamie's confusion is completely true to his
character and brilliantly imagined. A man must have a strong spirit
to stand fast to absolute, spiritual truths in the face of overwhelming
rational arguments. Living a transcendental life is most difficult;
and, although Jamie is a good boy, he is not a saint. Like most men's,
his character is flawed by the desire to preserve himself at all cost. As
has been observed, the conflict between selfishness and selflessness
runs throughout *A Cycle of the West*, as *The Song of Three Friends*
demonstrates. In *Poetic Values*, Neihardt points out that only in the
final stages of self-enlightenment can an ordinary person become extraordinary by merging his individual self with the cosmic All. Try as
he will, Jamie cannot reach that point; and he yields to Jules. They
flee, leaving Hugh without food and without weapons.

When Hugh awakens, he finds himself in a kind of Hell, for
without human comradeship, the world is meaningless. Hell for
Neihardt is not some mythical subterranean region; it lies within
each person. Hugh tries at first, to rationalize about the desertion
that has occurred; and he thinks that perhaps Jamie had good reason
for deserting. But rationality once again fails when faced by
monstrous evil. Just as Lear is driven mad by the irrational cruelty of
Goneril and Regan, Hugh is also driven mad by Jamie, even though
Jamie's evil was not deliberate. Once touched by evil, Hugh
becomes evil himself. Because his friend yielded to the devil within,

Hugh surrenders himself to the fires of vengeance. He forsakes his better nature, just as Othello does when instilled with Iago's green-eyed monster. At this moment Hugh becomes very much like Captain Ahab, the defiant man.

Just as the thirst for vengeance drives Ahab onward toward his meeting with Moby Dick, his desire leads Glass across the hostile plain. Hugh becomes an example of Albert Camus's metaphysical rebel, the man who says *no*; for, according to Camus, "Metaphysical rebellion is the movement by which man protests against his condition and against the whole of creation."[17] The metaphysical rebel, who "attacks a shattered world in order to demand unity from it," is a son of Cain who denies God and who asserts his own strength against God's omnipotence. The tragic hero, often such a man, is doomed by Fate; but he struggles against that doom and in his struggle finds a meaning for his life. Hugh Glass not only protests and attacks but finds such meaning in life.

At the beginning of Hugh's crawl, Neihardt introduces a theme which appears in several of his works — the Ghostly Brother — and that originated, as has been noted, in Neihardt's first vision. Although he was greatly moved by this early experience, he did not fully understand it until he was much older. In the early lyric, "The Ghostly Brother," Neihardt first presented the idea that there are two forces in every person's life, forces which he first discovered when he was only eleven years old. One force represents common sense and ordinary satisfactions; the other stands for higher longings, "the urgent obligation to give oneself away, to be lost in something impersonal and bigger than oneself; the conception of living as a process of progressive weaning."[18] In "The Ghostly Brother," these two forces are symbolized by the speaker of the poem and by his ghostly brother who represents his immortal longings. This imaginary brother calls out to the poet to break the bonds of earth and discover truths greater than the ones most people live by.[19] In *The Song of Hugh Glass*, Hugh must choose between these same two contending forces — selfishness and selflessness; he can live for himself or for Jamie. His first reaction to Jamie's betrayal is terrible hatred and crushing grief, but then he has a vision in which Jamie appears as a kind of ghostly brother who brings Hugh back to his better self, to his higher being:

> A retrospective vision of the lad
> Grew up in him, as in foggy night
> The witchery of semilunar light

Mysteriously quickens all the air.
Some memory of wind-blown golden hair,
The boyish laugh, the merry eyes of blue,
Wrought marvelously in the heart of Hugh,
As under snow the daemon of the Spring.
And momently it seemed a little thing
To suffer: nor might treachery recall
The miracle of being loved at all,
The privilege of loving to the end.
And thereupon a longing for his friend
Made life once more a struggle for a prize —

Indeed, Hugh's two struggles occur simultaneously as he crawls one hundred miles on his bloody hands and knees: the outer struggle is between Hugh Glass and a hostile wilderness; the inner one is between his selfish desire for revenge and his unselfish love for Jamie.

The crawl itself is one of the most remarkable passages in modern American poetry, for Neihardt describes the landscape as if it were a living thing. In Glass's fevered mind, each seemingly trivial event is charged with meaning; and Nature is the symbol of spirit. In its portrayal of human endurance under extreme stress, the section entitled "The Crawl" resembles a story, "To Build a Fire," by Jack London; but Neihardt adds the extra, transcendental dimension by also focusing on Hugh's inner struggle. The dry, parched, burning land is an outward manifestation of Hugh's own spiritual desolation. Deprived of the one thing which gave his life more than brute significance, Jamie's love, he must try to find help not only for his crushed body but also for his ravaged mind. Like a prophet wandering in the wilderness seeking God, Hugh also searches for signs of spiritual meaning. This religious message of selfless forgiveness is emphasized throughout "The Crawl," but Neihardt makes his point without preaching. Nature is here the moral teacher, just as it is in Romantic poetry. For example, Hugh finds an alkali sink, and its water, though tainted, offers some relief:

And yet, as may accrue
From specious love some profit of the true,
One gift of kindness had the tainted sink.
Stripped of his clothes, Hugh let his body drink
At every thirsting pore. Through trunk and limb
The elemental blessing solaced him;
Nor did he rise till, vague with stellar light,

> The lone gulch, buttressing an arch of night,
> Was like a temple to the Holy Ghost.

As he lies in the darkness, Hugh sees another vision of his ghostly brother Jamie. Though Jamie's love proved false, it was still love; and love has redeeming qualities for Hugh Glass, another man who loved "not wisely, but too well."

In his struggle for survival in the hostile wilderness which Neihardt, always a master at description, paints so well, Glass reverts to the animal, eating carion ripped away from a coyote. In the course of his crawl, he is reduced from a proud man with a spirit large as his giant frame to a blubbering child as layer after layer of his civilization is stripped away by pain and madness. But Glass, like the heroes of tragedy, is more than an ordinary man. He is a god in ruins, and he retains one last glimmer of humanity. He curses fate and feels sorry for himself, yet he still clings to "the fragment of a hope for crutch." Magnificent in adversity, he finally discovers the means to overcome the wilderness — a worn knife blade found in the ashes of an Indian campfire. With this tool, he rises from savagery to civilization, climbs from darkness into light. Neihardt, always concerned with the universal meaning of his epic, uses this incident as a symbol of man's rise. When Hugh seizes this knife, he is like Arthur pulling Excalibur from the stone.

When Hugh's ordeal is over, the tragedy is ready for its final resolution. Neihardt enforces this idea, perhaps needlessly, by introducing a chorus of half-wild Indian dogs who wail while Hugh sings by his triumphal fire. Up to this point, the poem has maintained the pattern of classical tragedy; for Hugh is a great man betrayed by a human flaw, not in himself but in another. As a lover scorned, he resembles Othello; as an old man beaten by youth, he resembles Lear; in his agony, he is blind Oedipus; in his thirst for revenge, he is Hamlet or Achilles. The winter wind reflects the intensity of his mood. When a man dedicates himself to violent revenge, he upsets the principle of order in the world and violates its spiritual harmony; and all is chaos: "White blindness grew black blindness — and 'twas night/Where through nor moon nor any star might grope."

When Hugh knocks at the gate of the fort, the pattern of the poem changes from tragedy to something beyond tragedy. Jules LeBon trembles in fear of Hugh's wrath, but Hugh explains that the man he wants is Jamie, who has gone down the river to Fort Atkinson. When Hugh finally catches him, Jamie lies dying in a Piegan lodge; and he cries for a priest to hear his confession. Hugh enters the lodge; but the poem, instead of ending in bloody vengeance, climaxes with redemption and thus achieves the sublimity which Neihardt found so compelling when he first heard the story of Hugh Glass. When Jamie tells his story to the man he thinks is a priest, he asks, "O Father, is there any hope for me?"; and the Black Robe answers that he remembers a similar case. After Jamie has eagerly asked what had happened, Neihardt ends the poem with a clever trick, which seems not that but an artistically satisfying conclusion; for the priest answers that one man in the similar case forgave, "For oh we have so short a time to live." At the sound of this familiar voice, Jamie suddenly realizes the truth:

> The gray of winter dawn
> Now creeping round the door-flap, lights the place
> And shows thin fingers groping for a face
> Deep-scarred and hoary with the frost of years
> Whereover runs a new springtide of tears.

> "O Jamie, Jamie, Jamie — I am Hugh!
> There was no Black Robe yonder — Will I do?"

In *The Song of Three Friends*, Frank Talbeau arrived too late to save Mike Fink from tragedy; but, in *The Song of Hugh Glass*, Neihardt moves beyond tragedy, thus keeping with his plan for *A Cycle* to progress "from the level of indomitable physical prowess to that of spiritual triumph in apparent worldly defeat" within the five epic songs. The reader understands this redemption, perhaps even experiences it for himself, because it is not given easily but is achieved by physical pain and mental suffering. In *The Song of Hugh Glass*, Neihardt turns a minor episode in the history of the American fur trade into a convincing poetic demonstration of man's best qualities; and, in so doing, he raises history to the level of myth. This feat is what Homer and Virgil achieved in the classic epics which Neihardt used as models; and, though one may not grant him the same immortality, one must applaud his achievements.

V   The Song of Jed Smith

The third song in *A Cycle*, *The Song of Jed Smith* (1941), was the last to be completed, and it fulfilled Neihardt's ambition to complete his epic by his sixtieth year. *The Song of Jed Smith* presents the exploits of the trapper and explorer who is also the central figure in

Neihardt's history, *The Splendid Wayfaring* (1920). Like its predecessor, the poem received critical praise, although its reviews were not quite as enthusiastic as those about the earlier epic songs. While the *Christian Century* critic wrote that the poem was "perhaps the strongest portrayal that has ever been given of this aspect of the American experience,"[20] the New York *Times* complained that Neihardt's trappers spoke like poets and philosophers. "This is the reason why an otherwise good plot is too much associated with reflections which disturb a theme that belongs to a primitive folk tale."[21]

The Song of Jed Smith is different from the other songs in several ways. First of all, instead of having an omniscient author as narrator, the narrative is related by three different characters, all trappers, who have been friends of Smith. By using this device, Neihardt hoped to get three different perspectives of his hero, which he does; but, in doing so, he surrenders power and concentration. One good thing that the use of three different characters as narrators accomplishes is the elimination of Neihardt's authorical asides, which had bothered some critics of the earlier poems. Another difference between *The Song of Jed Smith* and the other songs of *A Cycle* is Neihardt's use of language. The archaisms which sometimes marred the earlier poems have disappeared because such words would not be spoken by three trappers; instead, the language is more colloquial, sprinkled with an occasional "Aw hell." Neihardt, however, is able to use this colloquial speech without sacrificing poetry, for his trappers speak a language rich in frontier metaphor, and each has his own distinctive voice.

But the major difference between *The Song of Jed Smith* and the two heroic songs which precede it in *A Cycle* lies in the characters of their respective heroes. Mike Fink is brute man, selfish, boastful, and unredeemed; he kills and is in turn killed in accordance with the ancient law of blood for blood. Although Talbeau tries to save Mike at the end, he learns too late the virtue of forgiveness. Hugh Glass, who also begins as a brute, is mauled by a grizzly; and he uses his tremendous, animallike strength to crawl one hundred miles for help. But, unlike Mike Fink, Hugh Glass knows love; and it is that love which leads him to forgiveness and transcendence. Jed Smith is different, and he represents the third stage in Neihardt's history of the frontiersman. Fink and Glass are imperfect men; Jed Smith is perfect from the beginning. He is the apotheosis of the frontiersman, the final flowering, the ultimate development. He fits exactly D. H. Lawrence's famous definition of Cooper's Natty Bumppo as "a saint

with a gun." Like Natty, Smith combines the skills and the keen
shooting eye of a pathfinder with a philosopher's knowledge of his
place in the world and with a theologian's appreciation of God's
divine plan. But, since hagiography can be dull, its presence in this
poem is the principal flaw in *The Song of Jed Smith*. Because Smith
is perfect, his character does not develop like the others'; and he
never struggles with ordinary human temptations. If he were not
such a vigorous man of action, he would seem something of a prig.

By making Jed Smith into a sort of frontier saint, Neihardt
changes the spirit of his epic. The first two songs are Hellenistic
since the Ashley-Henry men are Argonauts, who, while larger than
life, nevertheless have human failings. *The Song of Jed Smith* is
Hebraic; each of the narrators seems like a disciple describing how
his favorite prophet led a chosen people into the Promised Land; the
Comanches fill the roles of Phillistines; and New Testament parallels
are also present, especially in the last lines of the poem:

> The bloody, feathered huddle that was Jed,
> Half buried in Comanches, coming to;
> The slow red trail, the hard, last trail that grew
> Behind him, crawling up the bank to seek
> The frightened horse; too dizzy sick and weak
> To make it past the sepulcher of shade
> The sandstone ledge and balanced bowlder made
> Against the swimming dazzle of the sun;
> The band returning for the horse and gun
> To find him there, still moaning, in his tomb
> And roll the bowlder on him.

By making Jed Smith a perfect person to begin with, Neihardt
eliminates the double conflict which adds an extra dimension to both
The Song of Three Friends and *The Song of Hugh Glass*. In these
two epics, man's struggle is, as has been observed, twofold — against
a hostile wilderness and against his own selfishness. These two
struggles Neihardt unites in his excellent descriptions in which the
landscape reflects the characters' emotions and is an outward
manifestation of their inner pain. But, since Jed Smith appears to
lack such human flaws, his struggle is only against the wilderness.

The Song of Jed Smith begins with a group of trappers seated
around a campfire at sunset. They are joined by a lone rider, old Bob
Evans; and the story telling begins. A trapper named Black recalls
the names of Smith's companions as if they constituted a roll of

heroes. Squire, the next speaker, is a relatively young man whose emphasis is on how Smith was different from other men. When Evans, the scholar of the group, explains that "He [Smith] has the humble wisdom that is wonder," Squire tries to explain this wonder in terms of unknown mountains and new rivers flowing to the sea. This "sense of wonder" is a basic characteristic of many classic American books, and it runs throughout *Jed Smith*.[22]

Black, for example, recalls how he crossed the Lost River Valley with Smith and in the process learned the meaning of faith. Though they are in desert country, Smith knows they will find water soon; and, when they do, he takes out his Bible for some "heavy reading." Here Neihardt is careful not to make Smith seem too pious, but he is a preacher nonetheless. This passage, however, is somewhat sentimentalized; and the attempt to make Black seem a tough-talking trapper with a heart of gold is not entirely successful:

> "Well, when he began
> To read out loud, 'twas not as parsons do.
> He said it just like anything that's true —
> 'The sun is shining,' maybe, or 'the birds
> Are singing.' Something got into the words
> That made them seem they couldn't be the same
> That you remembered. For the Lord became
> A gentle shepherd, real as Mr. Jones,
> And he had made us rest our weary bones
> In that green pasture by the waters there!"

Jed Smith is a kind of prophet leading his people through the wilderness; but, unlike many of the prophets, he never has a moment's doubt that God is on his side, and he never has to fight off temptations from world, flesh, or devil. If the magnitude of a man's struggle determines the value of his existence, as Neihardt demonstrates in many other works, then Jed Smith's value is less than that of other Neihardt heroes, for he seems somehow above the struggles of his ordinary followers. Like the figures on Keats's urn, Smith is "all breathing human passion far above." Even when his men cross the Mojave Desert and arrive in California, the first Americans to make California by land, he is strangely aloof and punctilious. As Black remembers,

> "And so," he chuckled, "there was Paradise,
> And all us lanky, ragamuffin scamps

A-faunching! What does 'Diah do? He camps
To shave his whiskers!''

Bob Evans, the most intelligent of the three narrators, because his
role is to explain Smith's special gift, fares better than the others, especially in his description of Smith's famous discovery of South Pass
which opened the West Coast to American settlers. Wandering in
winter, dangerously low on water, Smith still has faith; he is the True
Believer:

> "He spoke of water yonder where the day
> Was like a wild beast crouching for the leap
> Across the black wall. Wasn't time to sleep
> Until the horses drank. And when I said
> The rigmarole that grumbled in my head,
> How I'd believe in water that I saw,
> There came that flint-hard setting of the jaw,
> That long-range, hawk-gaze penetrating through you,
> The way you said, Art, — wondered if he knew you
> Or you knew him. And then his eyes went kind.
> 'That saying, Bob,' he said, 'is for the blind.
> Believing is a better way to see.' ''

In this passage, Neihardt has Bob Evans provide an excellent summary of what made Jed Smith the great explorer that he was. A True
Believer, absolutely convinced of his own rectitude, can accomplish
great things; but to do so he must pay a heavy price: he must
sacrifice his own humanity to the cause he serves, and Jed Smith
remains a solitary figure throughout the poem. The men admire him
to the point of worship, but they do not love him; and he does not
love any of them, except in the abstract sense of following God's
Commandment to love one's neighbor.

At only one moment does Jed Smith exhibit any normal human
emotion, and this moment is perhaps the best-dramatized episode in
the entire poem. His men think they see water, but it is only a
mirage. Bob Evans remembers that moment well:

> "One look at 'Diah told
> The answer that I knew. It was an old,
> Old man I saw a moment in his place,
> The look of something broken in his face
> That wasn't to be mended any more.
> I see that I had never known before
> How much I'd leaned upon him like a child,

Until he turned that face on me and smiled —
When nothing but the smile of it was Jed.
'You see, it's just beyond the salt,' he said,
'A little way.' And for a moment there,
Not anything but hearing Silas swear
Beneath his breath was left to fill the lack,
Until I saw that hawk-gaze coming back,
That long-range look of something that he saw
Beyond you; and the setting of the jaw
Was cruel in the face that it denied.
I didn't know how lean and hollow-eyed
It was until the light of it went dim,
That quicksand moment when I pitied him —
The leaner on his pity — even I!"

This excellent descriptive verse is lean, spare, and true. It has an authentic voice and ring to it, and it makes the reader see for just a moment the inward suffering of a seemingly perfect man.

But this passage is only one moment, and Smith quickly regains his composure. This composure is the difference between the passion of Jed Smith, who constantly sacrificed his own well being for his holy ideal — the filling in of the blank spaces on the map — and the passion of Jesus. The Pieta of Michelangelo moves those who see it with its suffering, its *human* love, which Jed Smith never reveals. Smith may be immortal, and a far worthier man than rough old Hugh Glass; but the reader cares for Glass in a way he cannot about the explorer. Nevertheless, Neihardt's portrayal of him is good and true; and *The Song of Jed Smith* is filled with the same epic description of hunger and thirst, of magnificent natural beauty and horrid natural ugliness, that runs throughout *A Cycle of the West*.

VI The Song of the Indian Wars

The last two books of *A Cycle*, *The Song of the Indian Wars* (1925) and *The Song of the Messiah* (1935), are Neihardt's finest poetic achievements. Written at the peak of his poetic skill, they deal with material which he had studied and written about for twenty years. His entire literary career until the time of their composition — the lyrics, the short stories, the early novels, and the nonfiction — was only preparation for these two epic songs. They are the fulfillment of a lifelong literary quest for a profound vision of the world, and they communicate that vision to the reader in poetry that is still fresh, vital, original, and charged with creative energy. Anyone who doubts that John G. Neihardt is a genuine American bard in the tradition of Walt Whitman needs only to have heard him recite "The Death of Crazy Horse" from *The Song of the Indian Wars* to have his doubts erased. For more than forty years, audiences at Neihardt's readings were moved by the power of his words, yet these poems still do not appear in the official teaching anthologies of American literature. They do belong there, however, because they stand comparison with any other American verse of this century. In fact, they are far superior to the dry exercises and little symbolic pieces which often pass for poetry. In these two epic songs, Neihardt takes big chances — and triumphs.

The Song of the Indian Wars covers the period from 1865 to the death of Crazy Horse in 1877; and its subject — the war between the Sioux and the United States Cavalry — is told from both sides but with obvious sympathy for the Indians. When the poem was first published, some of its reviews believed it deserved the Pulitzer Prize, an honor which Neihardt never received. Frank Luther Mott, a longtime admirer of Neihardt's work, was especially enthusiastic, and he praised the epic spirit of the poem and pointed out that the work also preserved "the human note."[23] Other critics praised the way Neihardt maintained a level of intensity throughout thousands of lines, and others commented on the fact that the poem had very few weak spots for a work of such length. Although this remarkable poem is seldom read today, the current revival of interest in American Indian history may — should — introduce *The Song of the Indian Wars* to a new generation of readers; moreover, it is now available in paperback.

Neihardt, who used several sources in writing the poem, had already spent years in research before he actually began to write. In his youth he had met Captain Grant March, who had commanded the steamer *Yellowstone* at the time of Custer's campaigns. He had also made friends with Curly, one of Custer's Crow Scouts and perhaps the only survivor of the famous "Last Stand." He also knew several old veterans of the Sioux Wars who told him their stories and who respected him enough to name him the only noncombatant member of the Order of Indian Wars. Neihardt also used secondary sources, particularly Charles Eastman's *Indian Heroes*, which contained the speeches of Red Cloud. But the poem is more than a retelling from historical sources, for Neihardt uses *The Song of the Indian Wars* to develop several of the major themes in *A Cycle*, themes which are also present in his other work.

One may have difficulty at first in seeing the link between *The*

Song of Jed Smith and *The Song of the Indian Wars* which follows it. Why, for instance, does Neihardt leave out more than forty years of history? In his preface to *A Cycle*, Neihardt explains that ". . . the five *Songs* are linked in chronological order; but in addition to their progress in time and across the vast land, those who feel as I have felt while the tales were growing may note a spiritual progression also — from the level of indomitable physical prowess to that of spiritual triumph in apparent worldly defeat. If any vital question be suggested in *The Song of Jed Smith*, for instance, there may be those who will find its age-old answer once again in the final Song of an alien people who were also men, and troubled."

The reader begins *A Cycle of the West* with Mike Fink and his friends, a gang of brawling, often insensitive louts, brave men but not particularly intelligent. Hugh Glass is both a spiritual and a physical man, while Jed Smith is a kind of frontier saint. Yet even the finest white men cannot match the spirituality of their Indian enemies. These "savages" are more admirable in almost every man than the so-called civilized men who covet their land. Yet Neihardt's Indians are not just idealized noble savages but flesh-and-blood people, memorable characters in what Neihardt believed was the last great drama in the history of Western man, his final push to the Pacific. In the first three songs of *A Cycle*, the reader sees the victors; now he witnesses the agony of the defeated. Though the Indians lose both their land and, often, their lives, the reader is left with one consolation — the spiritual truths expressed in their culture are not extinguished. They live on in a few old men like Black Elk, in a few younger people who refuse to follow the Wasichu way, and they live on in Neihardt's poetry.

The Song of the Indian Wars begins just after Appomattox; for, after being interrupted by the Civil War, the westward tide is ready to roll once more. Again, as in *The Splendid Wayfaring*, Neihardt emphasizes the universality of this theme — the relentless urge to move on:

> Again the bugles of the Race blew west
> That once the Tigris and Euphrates heard.
> In unsuspected deeps of being stirred
> The ancient and compelling Aryan urge.
> A homing of the homeless, surge on surge,
> The valley roads ran wagons, and the hills
> Through lane and by-way fed with trickling rills
> The man-stream mighty with a mystic thaw.

> That summer now the Mississippi saw
> What long ago the Hellespont beheld.

This Westward Movement Neihardt both applauds and regrets in *The Song of the Indian Wars*. On the one hand, it fulfills the destiny of the race and represents the triumph of Western civilization. Neihardt often brings out the best qualities of the migrants — their intelligence, their physical strength, their heroism, and their faith. On the other hand, the coming of pioneers who will plow the prairie and plant towns means the demise of the bison and the end of flourishing culture which is of equal, and perhaps one of greater value, to the one that replaces it. The white man, the European, the Aryan, or whatever name one chooses, is logical, rational, acquisitive, and a master of technology. The Indian is a spiritual man who has no technology, who has few marketable skills, and who uses land for hunting and for praying since his land is an integral part of his faith. By using this contrast throughout the poem, Neihardt emphasizes the theme of selfishness versus selflessness which runs through his entire *Cycle*. The American Indian does not understand the white man's drive to conquer the whole earth, nor does he understand the white man's urge to acquire more and more land, more and more wealth. Why must they lie? What compels them to come swarming out of the East?

This background prepares for Red Cloud's War, the first series of battles Neihardt dramatizes. In the summer of 1866, the government had completed a series of treaties with the Sioux; however, at new negotiations it now demands a road through the Powder River country to the newly discovered gold fields along the Madison. Many Sioux chiefs object, and Neihardt recreates their speeches to the treaty-makers at Fort Laramie. His ear for Indian speech is superb; even when he invents, instead of using verbatim accounts of what the chiefs said, every word seems authentic. A few years later, in *Black Elk Speaks*, he fooled experienced historians and anthropologists into thinking that speeches written entirely in his words were those of the old Sioux. The elevated language of Indian speech is also appropriate for a serious epic poem — more appropriate perhaps than the saltier speech of the trappers — because it is straightforward, dignified, and poetic. Here, for example, are the words of Spotted Tail, an uncle of Crazy Horse and a friend of the white man, as he tries to act as a conciliator:

> "Brothers, friends!"
> Slow words he spoke. "The longest summer ends,
> And nothing stays forever. We are old.
> Can anger check the coming of the cold?
> When frosts begin men think of meat and wood
> And how to make the days of winter good
> With what the summer leaves them of its cheer.
> Two times I saw the first snow deepen here,
> The last snow melt; and twice the grass was brown
> While I was living at the Soldier's Town
> To save my Brulés. All the while I thought
> About this alien people I had fought,
> Until a cloud was lifted from my eyes.
> I saw that some great spirit makes them wise.
> I saw a white Missouri flowing men,
> And knew old times could never be again
> This side of where the spirit sheds its load.
> Then let us give them the Powder River Road,
> For they will take it if we do not give.
> Not all can die in battle. Some must live.
> I think of those and what is best for those.
> Dakotas, I have spoken."

Such words are anathema to Red Cloud. His land cannot be bought with a few presents, because for him, as for Black Elk and for Eagle Voice in *When the Tree Flowered,* the land is Maka, Mother Earth. To see how Neihardt heightens Red Cloud's speech without changing its original purpose or character, one can compare a literal prose translation of his words with Neihardt's fine blank verse.

"Great white father sends us presents and wants new road. But White Chief goes with soldiers to steal road before Indian says yes or no!"[24]

> "These white men here have begged our hunting land.
> Their words are crooked and their tongues are split;
> For even while they feign to beg for it,
> Their warriors come to steal it! Let them try,
> And prove how good a warrior is a lie,
> And learn how Ogalalas meet a thief!"

The only word which seems at all false is "feign," but its use is the most minor of objections to an excellent speech.

Red Cloud, after striding out of Fort Laramie, meets other Sioux in council on the Powder River and makes an offering to his gods. Neihardt is always careful to stress the religious qualities of the Lakota way; for, even at their most warlike moments, the Sioux take time for religious observations. This religion, as *Black Elk Speaks* and *When the Tree Flowered* also indicate, is a unitary one in which all life is in harmony with the Spirit. The coming of the white man breaks the sacred hoop and violates the harmony of all things. The same force which makes the grass grow and the sun go down also controls man's destiny, but white men do not realize this fact of nature. As a result, they are separated from the natural world around them, as Sitting Bull explains very well:

> "They cut their land in pieces, fencing out
> Their neighbors from the mother of all men!
> When she is sick, they make her bear again
> With medicines they give her with the seed!
> All this is sacrilegious!"

This contrast between the organic world view of the Lakota and the mechanistic outlook of their conquerors is closely related to the theme of selfishness versus selflessness. If one sees land as a thing, then he can buy it, sell it, hoard it, or use it any other way he chooses. If, however, land is not property but a living force, Maka or Mother Earth, it cannot be the mere possession of one man; for all men have an equal right to enjoy the land and its fruits. To the rational white man, this view seems irrational; to the Indian, it is self-evident. Thus the Indian wars described in Neihardt's poem are more than battles over territory, which is the way most people usually think of them; they are contests between two ways of life. The tragedy is that only the Indians realize this contrast because the soldiers, the miners, and the farmers are too concerned with their manifest destiny to occupy the continent to worry about philosophy.

Most men are like the United States Cavalry, the Black Hills gold prospectors, and the farmers of prairie wheat. They take the meaning of their existence from things, and they measure success only in terms of material prosperity. This materialism is Neihardt's thesis in book after book, story after story, poem after poem; and, in his laureate address, he lectured the Nebraska legislature on the practicality of poetry, and in *Poetic Values* he speaks of the need for self-enlightenment. Until the white man can learn something of the Indian's spiritual awareness, the white man is only half a man.

After presenting the speeches in *Song of the Indian Wars*, Neihardt does an excellent job of dramatizing the charge of horses and the rain of arrows that occur in the battles. In the famous Fetterman Fight, Captain William Fetterman is tricked by Indian decoys into a trap which costs him, his eighty men, and two hundred braves their lives. In Neihardt's account, the rhythm quickens with short, choppy sentences as the cavalry charges to its death; and the poetry is full of clear, sharp images like this one: "A wheel-mule, sprouting feathers at his back,/Rears like a clumsy bird essaying flight/And falls to vicious kicking."[5] The reader hears the whoop of Lakota warriors and the cursing of the troopers. Then everything is strangely silent.

Shortly after this battle comes the fight at Beecher's Island, which one critic calls the best-written episode in the entire *Cycle*.[25] "Beecher's Island" begins with an evocative description of the gathering storm. In the confrontation of railroad with buffalo is a summary of the conflict between Lakota and Wasichu. The slow but inexorable progress of the railroad is like "an inchworm bound for San Francisco Bay." Then, as summer passes into fall, the cavalry pursues the Cheyenne warriors led by the epic-named Roman Nose; and the description of landscape is among Neihardt's best. As the cavalry passes,

> The buffalo, at graze
> Like dairy cattle, hardly deigned to raise
> Their shaggy heads and watch the horsemen pass.
> Like bursting case-shot, clumps of blue joint grass
> Exploded round them, hurtling grouse and quail
> And plover.

The troopers are suddenly attacked and pinned on an island in the dry bed of the Arikara River, and Roman Nose prepares for battle as an epic hero should. This passage is elevated poetry, yet extremely typical of the Cheyenne attitude toward warfare:

> He cast his robe away,
> Got up and took the bonnet from its case
> And donned it; put the death-paint on his face
> And mounted, saying, "Now I go to die!"
> Thereat he lifted up a bull-lunged cry
> That clamored far among the hills around;
> And dying men took courage at the sound
> And muttered, "He is coming."

This heroic chief leads a desperate charge with gallantry and valor but dies in the attempt: "So Roman Nose, the Flame of Many Roofs,/Flared Out." After his death, the battle becomes a siege, and the soldiers hope to get a message to the nearest fort. Suffering from hunger and thirst, they wait eight days. In his other epic songs, Neihardt dramatizes the struggle of man against nature; but the suffering in "Beecher's Island" is even more terrible because the men are unable to help themselves:

> The fourth sun since the battle lingered long.
> Putrescent horseflesh now befouled the air.
> Some tried to think they liked the prickly pear.
> Some tightened up their belts a hole or so.
> And certain of the wounded babbled low
> Of places other than the noisome pits,
> Because the fever sped their straying wits
> Like homing bumblebees that know the hive.
> That day the Colonel found his leg alive
> With life that wasn't his.

During the morning of the ninth day, desperate and without hope, Beecher's men are rescued in the best tradition of the United States Cavalry and the western movie. Neihardt's ending, however, is not false drama but historical truth.

The next section of *The Song of the Indian Wars* is entitled "The Yellow God," and it emphasizes the greed which brought prospectors into the Black Hills and George Armstrong Custer to protect them. The gold lust debases men and makes them all alike, "the hero and the coward and the fool." Instead of searching for a worthy grail, "the errant Galahad" is "mistaken in the color of the gleam." In contrast to the greedy gold seekers is the most remarkable character in Neihardt's entire epic, Crazy Horse. By juxtaposing the army of gold seekers with the army of Crazy Horse, Neihardt contrasts the worst representatives of white culture with the best representative of the Oglala Sioux, a man who in almost every way fits the definition of the perfect epic hero.

First of all, Crazy Horse is the most respected man of his entire tribe, although he is only about thirty years old. But he is not only a good warrior; he is also extraordinary because of his special intellectual quality. The "Crazy" in his name is actually a poor translation of the Sioux *witko*, which means "magic" or "enchanted" and which refers to his special vision (like Black Elk's). Because of this vision, he has achieved the perfect union of mind and body:

> What lonely vigils on a starry hill,
> What fasting in the time when boyhood dies
> Had put the distant seeing in his eyes,
> The power in his silence?

Crazy Horse leads his people in their last resistance against the tide of white settlement; and his battles, though often heroic, are like the struggle of one lonely man who is fighting the sea. His moment of sweetest victory occurs at the Battle of Little Big Horn, and Neihardt's account is excellent narrative verse. When Custer charges, he is "the Wolf of Washita," whose pack follows him. But Custer is met by another epic hero:

> It was Gall.
> A night wind blowing when the stars are dim,
> His big black gelding planted under him;
> And scarce he seemed a man of mortal race,
> His naked body and his massive face
> Serene as hewn from time-forgotten rock. . . .

Crazy Horse, with his "wizard eyes" and with a face "transfigured by a burning from within," leads his warriors to the slaughter. All is blood and noise.

Although the Lakota are victorious on the Greasy Grass, other soldiers arrive to avenge the rubbing out of Long Hair; and the Indians, relentlessly hounded, are finally driven into starvation and surrender. *The Song of the Indian Wars* ends with this tragedy. "The Death of Crazy Horse," which ends the song, is by any definition great poetry. These ten pages constitute Neihardt's best known and most popular poem, the one he was most often asked to recite at his public readings.

"The Death of Crazy Horse" begins in the troubled spring of 1877. Indians and whites alike wonder whether or not Crazy Horse will bring his people into Fort Robinson, and Neihardt contrasts his former glory with his present agony:

> Whoever spoke of Crazy Horse, still heard
> Ten thousand hoofs.
> But yonder, with the crow
> And kiote to applaud his pomp of woe,
> The last great Sioux rode down to his defeat.

Crazy Horse's tragic fall moves the reader to pity him as a proud man who once led a proud people who are now reduced to "twice a

thousand beggars." When Crazy Horse brings his starving people
into Fort Robinson, Neihardt's description captures their suffering,
which is both physical and spiritual:

> Then eerily began
> Among the lean-jowled warriors in the van
> The chant of peace, a supplicating wail
> That spread along the clutter of the trail
> Until the last bent straggler sang alone;
> And camp-dogs, hunger-bitten to the bone,
> Accused the heavens with a doleful sound;
> But, silent still, with noses to the ground,
> The laden ponies toiled to cheat the crows,
> And famine, like a wag, had made of those
> A grisly jest.

Throughout "The Death of Crazy Horse," Neihardt chooses exactly the right detail to make the reader feel, as well as understand,
his point. Brilliant image follows brilliant image as he works through
nature to spirit. The landscape and the animals both reflect the
agony of Crazy Horse and the terrible dilemma with which he is
faced. He would like to die a heroic death, fighting for his land,
resisting to the last; but, unlike many literary heroes, he has a higher
responsibility to his people: the nation's welfare is more important
than his personal honor. He has reached the point that few of
Neihardt's other heroes ever reach, and he has achieved this
knowledge through his pain. Yet, by giving up his own individuality,
he becomes a greater person; and, by following his change, the
reader's pity changes to sense of awe. Like Hugh Glass, Crazy Horse
moves beyond tragedy into sublimity: he transcends tragedy by living the life of the soul. Neihardt shows his turning point in one brief
instant:

> Ruefully he smiled,
> The doubtful supplication of a child
> Caught guilty; loosened the bonnet from his head
> And cast it down. "I come for peace," he said;
> "Now let my people eat." And that was all.

But that is not all, because the tragedy of Crazy Horse is doubled.
He gives up, surrenders his manly pride, so that his people may eat;
but there is no food! Doubly defeated, in August, 1877, he is roused
by hearing of Chief Joseph's brave resistance in Idaho and Montana;

the flame of honor once again burns within him; and he leaves Fort Robinson. When the soldiers find him in the camp of Spotted Tail, his uncle, where he lingers like a lost boy, not quite sure what he should do for his people, they persuade him to return to Fort Robinson for a parley. For a moment, he is given new hope, only to have it horribly dashed:

> There was a door flung wide.
> The soldier chief would talk with him inside
> And all be well at last!

The door leads to a jail cell. Crazy Horse suddenly realizes his awful fate: "O nevermore to neighbor with the stars/ Or know the simple goodness of the sun!" He breaks free, and a frightened soldier stabs him with a bayonet.

The last moments of this brave young man are among the most genuinely moving in modern American literature. Neihardt's poetry is dignified, noble, and without any trace of sentimentality; for Crazy Horse dies as he has lived, with honor. The language Neihardt gives him in his last speech is simple and straightforward, but it has great evocative power because of the poem which precedes it. In a few lines, this speech summarizes the tragedy of the Indian wars, and for that matter of all similar wars; for great poetry is universal:

> "I had my village and my pony herds
> On Powder where the land was all my own.
> I only wanted to be left alone.
> I did not want to fight. The Gray Fox sent
> His soldiers. We were poorer when they went;
> Our babies died, for many lodges burned
> And it was cold. We hoped again and turned
> Our faces westward. It was just the same
> Out yonder on the Rosebud. Gray Fox came.
> The dust his soldiers made was high and long.
> I fought him and I whipped him. Was it wrong
> To drive him back? That country was my own.
> I only wanted to be left alone.
> I did not want to see my people die.
> They say I murdered Long Hair and they lie.
> His soldiers came to kill us and they died."

After Crazy Horse's death, his mother and father take his body to bury in some secret place; and the poem ends with perfect elegiac lines:

Who knows the crumbling summit where he lies
Alone among the badlands? Kiotes prowl
About it, and the voices of the owl
Assume the day-long sorrow of the crows,
These many grasses and these many snows.

VII   The Song of the Messiah

A *Cycle of the West* concludes with *The Song of the Messiah*,
which Neihardt completed in 1935; and the first reviews of this
poem were quite favorable; William Rose Benet supported it for the
Pulitzer Prize, but Neihardt did not win.[26] The subject of this is the
Ghost Dance religion which resulted in the massacre at Wounded
Knee Creek in the winter of 1890 when John Neihardt was already
nine years old. As Neihardt observes in his preface, *A Cycle of the
West* has a spiritual as well as a temporal progression; and *The Song
of the Messiah* is the final stage. *A Cycle* begins with powerful men
of brute strength and stamina who are trying to wrest a living from
the wilderness and who maintain the nation's drive to the Pacific.
Some of these men, notably Hugh Glass and Jed Smith, have an intellectual aspect to their character; but, in Hugh's case, he does not
realize his capability until the end of the poem. Chief Crazy Horse
represents the perfect union of the two forces, physical and spiritual,
mind and body. In *The Song of the Messiah*, however, the time for
heroic deeds has ended. The beavers have long since left the
streams; the buffalo, the prairies. The mighty hunters, trappers, and
warriors are also gone; all that remains is their spirit. Although the
great hoop of the Sioux nation is broken and although the sacred tree
has withered, the vision of these things, like Black Elk's vision, still
lives; for its truth is immortal.

The Song of the Messiah also represents the final stage in the long
journey of western man. The frontier has disappeared, and the
United States has become an urban nation. Aryan man began in the
Near East; during the Renaissance, he tried to reach the East by sail-
ing to the West, but he eventually ran aground on Plymouth Rock.
Now the American, the last and greatest of all the westward-moving
Aryans, faces the Pacific with this long wandering complete at last.
As the theme of Walt Whitman's poem "Passage to India" indicates,
western man has finally — through his invention, energy, and
courage — completely subdued the physical universe. Now he needs
the spiritual resources of Eastern thought to complete his passage to
India and to return to his roots in what Whitman calls "primal
thought." Like the Transcendentalists, Neihardt works through

nature to spirit; he begins with Adamic, natural man and concludes with a vision of the world beyond this life.

The Lakota are not Brahmins, but the American Indian did have his origins in the Orient, and the Sioux way is as otherworldly as that of the Buddhist or the Hindu. In the western European's confrontation with the American Indian, he confronts the wisdom of the East; and thus the name "Indian" becomes less of a misnomer than it might seem. Only by combining western rationality and technical skill with eastern spiritual wisdom can a man become a whole person. Neihardt preaches this concept, in many different ways, in almost all his work.

At the beginning of *The Song of the Messiah*, the end of the world seems at hand. This metaphor works well on several levels, for it is now the end of the nineteenth century, the end of the frontier, and the end of the Lakota nation. Since the Lakota have a spiritual relationship with the physical earth, when the Lakota disappear, the earth will also die:

> The Earth was dying slowly, being old.
> A grandma, crouched against an inner cold
> Above scraped-up ashes of the dear,
> She babbled still the story of the year
> By hopeless moons; but all her bloom was snow.
> Mere stresses in a monody of woe,
> Her winters stung the moment, and her springs
> Were only garrulous rememberings
> Of joy that made them sadder than the fall.

Even the promised redemption of spring is empty when the tree of life is dead. "April is the cruelest month," says T. S. Eliot, and Neihardt expresses a similar idea in this poem. When hope is lost, spring seems a cruel cheat. As always in *A Cycle*, the landscape reflects the characters' emotional states:

> In the sloughs
> The plum brush, crediting the robin's news,
> Made honey of it, and the bumblebee
> Hummed with the old divine credulity
> The music of the universal hoax.

The Sioux, now confined to reservations, are denied their old life-giving relationship with their land. Greed, as Neihardt tells his readers often in *A Cycle*, is a killer. The Indians are not greedy; but,

in their hunger, they place bodily needs above those of the mind and
spirit. As a result of the white man's treachery, neither their bodies
nor their spirits receive nourishment:

> "There is no hope for us," the old men said,
> "For we have sold our mother to the lust
> Of strangers, and her breast is bitter dust,
> Her thousand laps are empty! She was kind
> Before the white men's seeing made us blind
> And greedy for the shadows they pursue.
> The fed-on-shadows shall be shadows too
> Their trails shall end in darkness. . . ."

The Sioux are desperate men. Dying of hunger, they have lost the
will to fight because their nation has been broken up and their
heroes are all dead. A people must have some controlling ideal, some
myth, if they are to sustain their national vitality. In Eliot's *The
Waste Land*, the poet examines a modern world which has lost its
faith and now has nothing with which to replace it; and this same
fate has befallen the Sioux. But they cling to one last hope: some
have heard a rumor of a certain Paiute named Wovoka, who claims
to be the reborn Messiah and who will save the Indian. As has been
noted, this interaction between Christianity and other religions is a
lifelong interest of Neihardt's. In his first epic, *The Divine Enchantment*, he tells a Hindu story with obvious Christian parallels. The
Ghost Dance religion of Wovoka, except for a difference in the form
of worship, is entirely Christian in its theology. Wovoka preaches
nonviolence and brotherly love, and he asserts that he alone can bring
redemption. The Indians had, by this time in the late nineteenth
century, often been exposed to Christian missionaries; but, whether
they were Christian or not, Wovoka offered a creed in which the Indians could believe, one that they needed to believe; and he made
converts rapidly.

The form of this Ghost Dance religion was simple enough.
Wovoka claimed that he had died, gone to Heaven, and talked with
God. Now he was Christ reborn as an Indian, and he had a special
dance which would restore them to their former greatness. Wovoka
also prescribed a special costume, the Ghost Shirt painted with symbolic designs, to be worn during the dance. The people dancing the
Ghost Dance according to Wovoka's directions would see their dead
relatives and talk to them. Soon another world was coming in which
these dead would return and all the buffalo along with them. The

white men would disappear, either in a whirlwind or by being miraculously buried.

To learn more about this new religion, the Sioux sent emissaries to hear the new Messiah; and the stories they tell when they return take up most of the first part of *The Song of the Messiah*. Good Thunder is the first to speak. His account resembles a combination of Christianity with the Sioux belief in vision experiences. The symbol of the flowering tree at the center of the nation's hoop is, according to Good Thunder, present in the new religion because Wovoka saw such a vision while he was in the spirit world. In this passage, Neihardt demonstrates how the Sioux desperately wished for a restoration of their old way and a revitalization of their old religious symbolism, just as Black Elk wished for fulfillment of his vision, whose central symbol is also this magnificent tree:

> A tree whose leafage filled the living blue
> With sacred singing; and so tall it 'rose,
> A thousand grasses and a thousand snows
> Could never raise it; but all trees together,
> When warm rains come and it is growing weather
> And every root and seed believes,
> Might dream of having such a world of leaves
> So high in such a happiness of air.

Kicking Bear, another of the emissaries to Wovoka, emphasizes the Christian resurrection in his report to the tribe, one which is based by Neihardt on historical fact. When Kicking Bear actually examined the Paiute Messiah to see if he had the wounds of Christ on his body, he did find scars.

> "I tell you He is Jesus come again!
> I saw the marks upon Him! It is so!
> Have not the Black Robes told how long ago
> One came to save the people? It is He!
> Did not Wasichus nail Him to a tree?
> Did they not torture Him until he died?
> I saw the spear-wound bleeding in His side!
> His lifted palms — I saw them white with scars!"

Although many Sioux actually believed in Wovoka's message, some, including Sitting Bull, were skeptical. This skepticism is another version of the modern problem of belief which concerns

Neihardt not only in this poem but in many other works as well.
How can man exist without a faith, and yet how can anyone believe
in dead gods? And, if the old gods are dead, with what shall the nation replace them? Shall the nation worship the dollar, as Neihardt
asserts Americans do? And how can one determine the difference
between a genuine vision and a hallucination? These are the kind of
questions that Neihardt faces in *The Song of the Messiah*.

After the glowing reports of their ambassadors to Wovoka, the
Sioux begin to dance. But the Holy Tree they shuffle around and
around is only a sapling cottonwood, and the ritual is only an empty
form. The reader contrasts this useless ceremony with the still-vital
Sun Dance described in *The Song of the Indian Wars*. Some Indians
do have visions while dancing the Ghost Dance, but their dreams are
in vain; for the order comes from the white authorities that the dancing must cease — because anything that brings Indians closer
together and restores their lost faith constitutes a threat to the
United States Army. Even though the Ghost Dance is Christian in all
but its form of worship, and is completely nonviolent, the Indian
agents see it as a movement for Indian solidarity and as a direct
challenge to their authority; and the soldiers are sent to the reservations.

When the soldiers arrive, one of their chief targets is Sitting Bull,
the last of the great chiefs, who has returned from Canada and now
lives peacefully at Standing Rock. Because he is the last hero, the
United States government has been trying for years to find a reason
to capture him. As Neihardt imagines him on the evening of his
murder by Indian police sent to arrest him on orders from General
Miles, who is afraid of a new uprising, Sitting Bull has a mature, intelligent outlook on life; and he shares his wisdom with a friend. In
his speech, the values of the Indian are contrasted with those of his
oppressor. Sitting Bull is a prophet who knows that those who abuse
the earth are condemned by their own greed. He is a nineteenth-
century ecologist; and Neihardt, writing in the twentieth century,
saw that his vision was coming true:

> "Have I not seen the only mother, Earth,
> Full-breasted with the mercy of her Springs,
> Rejoicing in her multitude of wings
> And clinging roots and legs that leaped and ran?
> And whether winged or rooted, beast or man,
> We all of us were little ones at nurse.
> And I have seen her stricken with a curse

> Of fools, who build their lodges up so high
> They lose their mother, and the father sky
> Is hidden in the darkness that they build;
> And with their trader's babble they have killed
> The ancient voices that could make them wise.
> Their mightiest in trickery and lies
> Are chiefs among them."

This passage summarizes Neihardt's social, political, economic, and religious ideals. Coming as it does near the end of his epic, his message to the world is not preached but proved through the actions of his characters. Neihardt believes that man often debases himself to bodily needs at the expense of his mind or spirit. Bodily satisfaction is not bad; but a complete man must life a unified life in which the body and the spirit, the Me and the Not Me, or Nature and the Soul (Emerson's basic division in *Nature*), must work in harmony. If man misuses Nature, he will eventually deprive himself of her bounty; and, if one rich country tries to hoard all its goods and its food, the hungry masses in other countries will rise and conquer it. The same principle holds true for the poor within a nation's borders; for Neihardt, who was himself born poor, knew well the gnawing tooth of poverty.

The Sioux way must not be forgotten by readers because the Sioux realized these fundamental truths and lived accordingly. Their lives were harmonious and unified because they regulated their behavior according to these universal laws. Sioux parents, for instance, never inflicted corporal punishment; they almost never spoke harshly to their children because the children learned how to live by their parents' example. Anyone who violated a law broke the nation's hoop a little, so all members of the tribe worked to keep the hoop intact.

The Lakota were certainly a vigorous people, and they trained their young men to be strong and courageous fighters; but they also stressed that a man's function was to serve his vision. A good hunter who kept all his meat for himself and a good warrior who did not share his glory with the tribe would be frowned upon because such selfishness violated the unity of life. The Sioux had an organic view of life in which all living things were related and lived in natural harmony. No Sioux ever killed a buffalo, sliced out its tongue, and left the rest to rot; for such an act they would consider a crime against nature. Although the white man committed such sins, he seemed to prosper nevertheless. Only in the present era has his punishment arrived.

The tragedy of *The Song of the Messiah* is that only a few people realize these truths; for the rest continue their sins and their ignorant, shameful killing. Sitting Bull is shot by Indian police, betrayed by his own people; the old horse he rode in Buffalo Bill's Wild West Show thinks the shots are signals, and he starts to do his tricks. Next morning, the dawn itself reflects the passing of an era:

> Like the leaden ache
> Of some old sorrow, dawn began to break
> Beneath the failing star. And then — *he came!*
>
> Gigantic in a mist of moony flame,
> He fled across the farther summits there,
> That desolation of an old despair
> Illumined all about him as he went.
> And then, collapsing, like a runner spent,
> Upon the world-rim yonder, he was gone.

The Song of the Messiah ends with the massacre at Wounded Knee, one of the most ignominious chapters in American history. Sitanka's band, traveling under a white flag while their chief lies wounded in an ambulance, is returning to Pine Ridge Reservation because Sitanka hopes to find protection there from the soldiers sent to arrest him as a troublemaker. The three-hundred-and-fifty men, women, and children are surrounded by the Seventh Cavalry and ordered to give up their arms, but the troopers find only two rifles among them. Suddenly a shot rings out; the cavalry open fire with machine guns; and almost three hundred Indians are slaughtered, but twenty-five soldiers die from their own crossfire. Neihardt's description is brilliant throughout; and he first makes his readers share the suffering of Sitanka's followers, especially the pain of biting cold and gnawing hunger. As he does elsewhere in the poem, he uses a religious metaphor:

> The frail flesh, crucified,
> Forgot the Spirit. Truth was in the storm,
> And everlasting. Only to be warm,
> Only to eat a little and to rest,
> Only to reach that Haven of the Blest
> Amid the badlands!

Sitanka tries to give them some hope; he prays for wisdom, and he tells his people of a dream in which he finds some solace. He sees, he tells them, that they must learn to love the soldiers:

> Pray to understand
> Not ours alone shall be the Spirit Land.
> In every heart shall bloom the Shielding Tree,
> And none shall see the Savior till he see
> The stranger's face and know it for his own.

The next day, Sitanka awakens to a bugle call and the rumble of hooves. In the battle, he sees a soldier about to smash him with a rifle butt; and he suddenly receives a vision which provides some small consolation for the massacre; for, although the Lakota may die, the truth of their vision will endure. Neihardt expresses this truth brilliantly in Sitanka's last moment on earth:

> For a span,
> Unmeasured as the tragedy of man,
> Brief as the weapon's poising and the stroke,
> It burned upon him; and a white light broke
> About it, even as a cry came through
> That stabbed the world with pity. And he knew
> The shining face, unutterably dear!
> All tenderness, it hovered, bending near,
> Half man, half woman, beautiful with scars
> And eyes of sorrow, very old — like stars
> That seek the dawn. He strove to rise in vain,
> To cry "my Brother!"
>
> And the shattered brain
> Went out.

CHAPTER 6

The Everlasting Word

TO assess the value of a contemporary author's work is always difficult since the only true test of greatness is time. But John Neihardt's best poetry and prose wear well and appear to be gaining in popularity. The University of Nebraska Press has reissued all of his major work in paperback, and the publishing history of *Black Elk Speaks* indicates the continuing popularity of that fine book. Neihardt became a national celebrity in 1972 as a result of his television appearances on the "Dick Cavett Show," at which he demonstrated that he was still a dramatic reciter of his own poetry. At the time of his death, he was working on a second volume of his autobiography; the first volume, *All Is But a Beginning* (1972) had received excellent reviews.

Neihardt's best books have refused to die, not only because they are artistically successful but because they also deal with questions of acute concern to many people. A number of best-selling books of the past decade, including *The Making of a Counter-Culture* by Theodore Rozak and *The Greening of America* by Charles Reich, have postulated that a new culture is now thriving in the United States — a youth culture that rejects conspicuous consumption, advocates a return to the natural, and rebels against the politics of greed. As shallow as the culture may be, it does exist. Although the long, slow end of the Vietnam War and current economic and political conditions may have temporarily quenched the ardor of the counter-culture, such publications as *Mother Earth News* indicate that it still exists, although perhaps in a different form.

Neihardt addresses himself to these "young people," some of whom are not young, in the last chapter of his recently published memoir, *All Is But a Beginning*. He claims that the generation gap does not exist, and that he is on the side of the latest generation that, according to him, is "caught up in the greatest social revolution the world has ever known." In the "hirsute excesses" of the young, he says, "there is more than frivolity and fashion."[1] Neihardt's analysis of the world in which Americans live, with its poverty and misery within sight of plenty, with its senseless wars and its empty materialism, concludes with the observation that those who reject it are correct.

Neihardt's books, in contrast, assert the dignity and worth of the individual, the value of heroic struggle against an oppressor or against the oppressor in oneself, and the need for preserving what is left of natural beauty. He repeatedly attacks greed and proves that it is self-defeating. His works are religious, but they do not endorse any established church or any codified theology. He shares with the counter-culture a fascination for the mystical religions of the Orient and the native mysticism of the American Indian.

One may verify these assertions about the temper of our times simply by examining the paperback shelves in any large university bookstore. There he will find books on Hinduism and Buddhism (though the Zen wave has receded, yoga is increasing in popularity), volumes dealing with various sorts of mysticism, and whole walls lined with science fiction that blends mysticism with technology. The more popular novels are often those dealing with vision experiences or mystical searches — Herman Hesse's *Siddhartha* and Carlos Castenada's Don Juan books (which may be considered as novels) are good examples. And, in recent years, the bookstores have reserved a whole shelf for books about American Indians. The Western movie enjoys continued popularity, but now the Indian sometimes becomes the hero. *Little Big Man,* a film made from Thomas Berger's novel, features Old Lodge Skins, a Cheyenne who speaks like a "pop" version of Black Elk.

Critic Leslie Fiedler calls this new emphasis on the Indian "the return of the vanishing American"; and, in his recent book by that title, he discusses the sudden increase in new sorts of Westerns, ones which turn the old popular conventions into serious art. Fiedler sees this development as a return to a basic American myth in which the West and the Indian fill a longing in mankind for return to the primitive — an easy way out of twentieth-century difficulties. To Fiedler, the Western is a version of the pastoral in which the hero can avoid his responsibilities; and D. H. Lawrence makes the same comments about Cooper's Leatherstocking tales in his famous *Studies in Classic American Literature.* Fiedler also asserts that, sentimental though this idea may sometimes be, it "has haunted all

Americans, in their dreams at least if not in their waking consciousness; for it is rooted in our profound guilt; our awareness that we began our national life by killing something vital to the New World as well as something essential to the Old. . . ."[2]

Another writer deeply concerned with this lost vitality is Frank Waters (born 1902) who lived among New Mexico Indians and who celebrates the Pueblo way in both fiction and nonfiction — books which have also been recently released in paperback. Perhaps because he is himself one-eighth Cheyenne, perhaps because he actually lived and worked among Pueblos and Navahos, and perhaps because of his literary ability, Waters gets as close as any modern American writer besides Neihardt to the special qualities which make Indian life valuable. His best-known novel, *The Man Who Killed the Deer*, is the story of a young man named Martiniano who leaves his pueblo for the white man's school. When he returns, he discovers he can neither accept the old ways of life nor adopt new ones. He tries the peyote offered him by the Native American Church, but his artificially induced vision seems false to him, just as the Ghost Dance formulas seem false to Black Elk and to Sitting Bull.

The white man's church with its phallic steeple is also a meaningless form; and the pueblo kiva, a soft, rounded female form which symbolizes fertility, is for him only "a creed of supplication and appeasement." His friend Palemon gives him some advice which might have come straight from John Neihardt: he must learn to reconcile the needs of his mortal body with those of his immortal spirit and find a form of life that can provide harmony and unity. Not until the novel's end does Martiniano realize that lack of faith is his real problem. He decides to have his baby son adopted into a kiva and comes to understand the full meaning of the Pueblo religion. Like the Indian heroes of Neihardt's poetry, he is a Transcendentalist who works through nature to spirit. Waters closes with a metaphor which could have come right out of Emerson: "And he knew now that there is nothing killed, nothing lost, if one looks far or deep or high enough to see how its transmuted meaning is imparted for all men to read and understand. Ai. A man drops but a pebble into the one great lake of life, and the ripples spread to unguessed shores, to congeal into a pattern even in timeless skies of night."[3]

This theme is also found in Neihardt's work. Neihardt's Indians are, first of all, people who share feelings and attitudes with people of all times and places. They differ from other people, however, because their way of life provides what many men and women lack — an orderly, harmonious existence in which mind and body, nature and the soul, play equal parts. Like the best writers, Neihardt presents the reader with a complete world that is populated by unforgettable characters of all ages who exhibit the full range of human possibilities from heroism to cowardice, from charity to greed, from faith to hypocrisy. His epics celebrate the best qualities of Americans, and they demonstrate the tragic consequences of their worst crimes. Neihardt shows his readers the grand sweep of the Missouri River Valley from Kansas to the Rockies and demonstrates how that land shaped the men who lived on it. Above all, he has created works of literary art which communicate, without preaching or lecturing, a profound vision of the good life.

In the last chapter of *All Is But a Beginning,* Neihardt imagines a conversation with a cynical young man who asks him, "What's good about this absurd predicament in which we find ourselves? We don't know whence we came; we don't know whither we are bound."[4] In answer to this question, Neihardt presents four concepts which make life valuable and which he celebrates in his work. The first of these good things is love. Neihardt's early lyrics are love poems, sometimes unsure of themselves, sometimes even mawkish; but later he learned better ways of dramatizing love. In *The Song of Hugh Glass,* the best example, love transforms a grizzled old trapper into a man of sensitivity and understanding. When Hugh's love for Jamie finally leads him to forgive Jamie's selfish desertion, Hugh achieves nobility; he is a saint without seeming sanctimonious.

The love expressed in *The Song of the Indian Wars* and *The Song of the Messiah* is of a different kind — the love of a nation for its land is spiritual and transcends time. From their beginnings to the massacre at Wounded Knee, the Sioux loved their country and expressed that love in their name for it, Maka, Mother Earth, the principle of life. The Sioux, like other people, also love one another, as Neihardt demonstrates in *When the Tree Flowered.* This love is often shown in the parents' refusal to discipline their children harshly. Indeed, the children need no discipline because they understand the importance of both family and tribe; not to love one's land or one's people would break the nation's hoop. The greed which costs the Sioux their land is the absence of love.

Besides these kinds of love, Neihardt also portrays the love between man and woman. When Eagle Voice buries Tashina in the moving finale of *When the Tree Flowered,* he demonstrates his deep, abiding, and passionate love for his wife by placing his sacred quirt between her breasts. In the short stories "Mignon" and "Vylin," Neihardt describes the conflict of cultures when an Indian loves a white; and he realistically shows that sometimes not even love can transcend such differences.

Neihardt's second saving value is the satisfaction of the instinct of workmanship, and he proves the value of pride in one's craft by the pattern of his own life. He began his literary career as a word-drunk boy grinding out epics while he labored in the fields. He paid for his education — the Latin that he loved and that gave him necessary philosophical and literary background — by ringing the college bell. For thirty years he worked at *A Cycle of the West,* all the while teaching, writing book reviews, and giving recitations to support his family. But he always stuck to his job with a determination to see it through. Because he knew how to work, how to write and rewrite and rewrite again until the lines met his demanding standards, he became a master of poetic form who used every possible literary device to enliven his poetry and prose. He learned how to use rhythm, "the conscious manipulation of sound," and also how to make the form of his work reflect its function. Thus his best poetry fulfills Emerson's test of great poetry, "not meters, but a meter-making argument."

Closely related to Neihardt's insistence on the value of work is his belief that life is worthless unless people are willing to struggle. Without a goal, man has nothing for which to live. Neihardt's works often portray men struggling against a hostile nature in order to wrest a living from the wilderness. Hugh Glass's crawl, the steadfast exploration of Jed Smith, and the flight of the Lakota after the Battle of Little Big Horn are good examples. *The River and I* describes how young John Neihardt tested himself against the mighty Missouri and, in the process, learned firsthand what heroes the fur trappers must have been. But man's goal must be worthy and unselfish, for his relentless pursuit of gold in *Life's Lure* and *The Song of the Indian Wars* leads to his betrayal of his better nature.

Neihardt's third principle is that "the exaltation of expanded awareness in moments of spiritual awareness is good."[5] Neihardt experienced his first vision at the age of eleven, and most of his works are concerned with the search for some visionary gleam. *Black Elk Speaks* is one of the most remarkable versions of the vision experience in all literature, and it remains Neihardt's best-known and most popular work. In *Black Elk Speaks* and in *The Song of the Messiah,* the vision remains long after the nation's hoop has been broken by greed. In Black Elk's vision, the world is glorified, and the tree at the center of the nation's hoop blooms with hope and beauty. The power of this vision-experience allows man to transcend his earthly limitations and to get a glimpse of immortality that enables him to return to earth refreshed and with a clear knowledge of his destiny. Neihardt, like the American Transcendentalists, works through nature to the spiritual facts which natural facts symbolize. The reader of his poetry makes the imaginative leap from mortality into immortality.

Neihardt's fourth virtue is deep sleep. To illustrate, he quotes from *The Song of Jed Smith:*

> "There's something that you touch,
> And what you call it needn't matter much
> If you can reach it. Call it only rest,
> And there is something else you haven't guessed —
> The Everlasting, maybe. You can try
> To live without it, but you have to die
> Back into it a little now and then.
> And maybe praying is a way for men
> To reach it when they cannot sleep a wink,
> For trouble."

Neihardt then explains the fundamental theme in all his work: "that each 'good' involves the loss of self in some pattern larger than self." He tries to find literary equivalents for such patterns, for only in the loss of self in a greater whole does man find his true self. In reading Neihardt's poetry and major prose, one follows the path to Nirvana that he sets forth in *Poetic Values.* First comes "The Waking Consciousness" "in which men vividly conceive themselves as individuals and are exclusively aware of everyday experiences." This level is the one on which most people live; they conduct "practical" searches for the material goods necessary to live a comfortable existence; and they destroy what is best in themselves by seeking even more. Mike Fink, in *The Song of Three Friends,* is a good example of such a person.

The second stage is that of Dream-Sleep in which the individual self can take on many forms and be in a state of readiness such as that experienced by Black Elk and Eagle Voice when they received their visions. The third state is Deep Sleep: "Therein the illusory sense of individuality is lost, with all its suffering, merged in Brahman." In this ultimate state of Transcendental awareness, which Walt Whitman describes in "Song of Myself," the self is united with the soul; and it becomes, in Emerson's words, "part or parcel of God."[6] For one brief moment at the Battle of Wounded Knee, Sitanka experiences this state; but, at that very moment, a soldier's gun butt crushes his skull. Then, *A Cycle of the West* ends with three lines that make a fitting conclusion to all of Neihardt's work: "The mounting blizzard broke. All night it swept/The bloody field of victory that kept/The secret of the Everlasting Word."

A final assessment of Neihardt's contributions to literature must recognize that not all his work achieves the level of *Black Elk Speaks*, *When the Tree Flowered*, and the better sections of *A Cycle of the West*. His early lyrics are marred by excessive sentimentality, and only a few seem likely to endure. The two early novels fail because Neihardt, at that stage of his career, did not understand the novelist's technique; and the good, tight construction of the early stories is missing. Because of these apprentice works, one should not dismiss Neihardt, nor should one disregard *A Cycle* for its occasional defects of language and characterization.

At his best, Neihardt is an outstanding writer. His contributions to the literature of and about the American Indian are greater than those of any other novelist or poet. Because he understood the Indian so well, from years of living among them and from his voluminous reading in western history, he was able to write of them as individuals, not as "noble savages" or as living demonstrations of some anthropological thesis. He was also able to see the larger significance of their actions; and he demonstrates in his epic poetry that the westward movement was more important than the fall of Troy and just as heroic. The blank verse of this epic is often excellent, rich in metaphor, and suitable in its rhythms to the action described. In *A Cycle of the West* and in many of his later prose works, Neihardt reveals a literary craftsmanship developed through long years of patient labor.

Neihardt's criticism, now almost unknown, constitutes a defense of poetry for this era. Though it may seem old-fashioned, it demonstrates his integrity and his steadfast insistence that literature must not be debased by using it for propaganda or for any other purpose than the revelation of the writer's insight into character and his re-creation of life. In this criticism and in his stories and poems, Neihardt places himself in the organic tradition of Emerson, Thoreau, and Whitman. Although his work is not as great as theirs, he, like them, asks the reader to work through Nature to Spirit and to discover thereby that life offers more than its surface reality.

Perhaps the best ways to judge the lasting value of Neihardt's fiction, history, and poetry is to apply his own definition of the poetic symbol to what he wrote. In the *Laureate Address,* he defined the symbol as "a little door opened suddenly upon long vistas of life; and he who walks through them shall be glorified by the consciousness of his close kinship with all men in all time." The reader of *Black Elk Speaks* can experience the profound vision of an Oglala Sioux holy man, and the reader of *A Cycle* can share in the American epic by suffering vicariously through the crawl of Hugh Glass, the desert journey of Jed Smith, and the massacre at Wounded Knee. Americans can understand what impelled these men, both red and white, to feats that are now part of this country's folklore.

Notes and References

Chapter One

1. *All Is But a Beginning* (New York, 1972), p. 4.
2. *The River and I* (Lincoln, Nebraska, 1968), p. 4.
3. *All Is But a Beginning*, p. 15.
4. *A Cycle of the West* (New York, 1949), pp. vii - ix.
5. *All Is But a Beginning*, p. 48.
6. *Lyric and Dramatic Poems* (Lincoln, Nebraska, 1965), p. 163.
7. *All Is But a Beginning*, p. 48.
8. Ibid., p. 75.
9. *The Song of Three Friends* (New York, 1919), p. viii.
10. Julius T. House, *John G. Neihardt, Man and Poet* (Wayne, Nebraska, 1920), p. 16.
11. Ibid., p. 21.
12. Lucile Aly, "The Word-Sender: John G. Neihardt and His Audiences," *Quarterly Journal of Speech* 43 (April, 1957), 151.
13. Ibid., p. 153.
14. Ibid., p. 151.
15. *Laureate Address* (Chicago, 1921).
16. Wright Morris, "Remembrance of Cranks Past," *Time*, October 18, 1971, pp. 88 - 89.
17. F. Scott Fitzgerald,*This Side of Paradise* (New York, 1920), p. 282.
18. Review of *A Farewell to Arms* by Ernest Hemingway, St. Louis *Post-Dispatch*, September 28, 1929.
19. Review of *Dubliners* by James Joyce, St. Louis *Post-Dispatch*, December 18, 1926.
20. Review of *A Medieval Childhood* by Sherwood Anderson, St. Louis *Post-Dispatch*, December 20, 1926.
21. Review of *In Dubious Battle* by John Steinbeck, St. Louis *Post-Dispatch*, March 8, 1936.
22. Review of *The Great Tradition* by Granville Hicks, St. Louis *Post-Dispatch*, September 24, 1933.
23. Edgar Lee Masters, "Lucinda Matlock," in *Selected Poems* (New York, 1925), p. 387.

24. Edwin Arlington Robinson, "Credo," in *Collected Poems* (New York, 1937), p. 94.

25. Robert Frost, "The Need of Being Versed in Country Things," in *Complete Poems* (New York, 1967), p. 300.

26. Horace Traubel, *With Walt Whitman in Camden* (New York, 1914), III, 25 - 26.

27. Ralph Waldo Emerson, *Nature,* in *Selections from Ralph Waldo Emerson,* ed. Stephen E. Whicher (Boston, 1957), p. 31.

28. Henry David Thoreau, *Walden* and *Civil Disobedience,* ed. Sherman Paul (Boston, 1957), p. 128.

29. Louis Sullivan, *Kindergarten Chats and Other Writings* (New York, 1947), p. 32.

30. Charles Ives, *Essays Before a Sonata, The Majority and Other Writings,* ed. Howard Boatwright (New York, 1962), p. 71.

31. Thoreau, *Walden,* p. 227.

32. *Laureate Address,* p. 15.

33. Emerson, *Nature,* in Whicher, p. 22.

34. Ibid., "The Poet," p. 225.

35. *Laureate Address,* p. 43.

36. Ibid., pp. 43 - 44.

37. Matthew Arnold, "The Function of Criticism at the Present Time," in *Poetry and Criticism of Matthew Arnold,* ed. A. Dwight Culler (Boston, 1961), p. 257.

38. *Poetic Values: Their Reality and Our Need of Them* (New York, 1925), p. 13.

Chapter Two

1. *Lyric and Dramatic Poems* (Lincoln, Nebraska, 1965), p. v.

2. Ibid., p. v.

3. Agnes C. Laut, review of *A Bundle of Myrrh* by John G. Neihardt, New York *Times,* February 15, 1908, p. 83.

4. Anon., "Three Young Poets," *The Outlook* 89 (May 30, 1908), 261 - 62.

5. "Lines in Late March," in *Lyric and Dramatic Poems,* p. 1. All other citations of Neihardt lyrics are from this edition.

6. Bliss Carman, review of *Man Song* by John G. Neihardt, New York *Times,* November 20, 1909, p. 724.

7. Justine Leavitt Wilson, review of *Man Song, Book Review Digest* (1909), p. 329.

8. Anon., review of *The Stranger at the Gate* by John G. Neihardt, *Literary Digest* 44 (March 19, 1912), 549.

9. See Louis Marx, *The Machine in the Garden: Technology and the Pastoral Ideal in America* (New York, 1964).

10. *All Is But a Beginning,* p. 170.

11. House, p. 37.

12. *Poetic Values: Their Reality and Our Need of Them*, pp. 25 - 26.

13. Richard Crowder, "The Emergence of E. A. Robinson," *South Atlantic Quarterly* 45 (1946), 89.

14. Roy Harvey Pearce, *The Continuity of American Poetry* (Princeton, New Jersey, 1961), pp. 253 - 55.

Chapter Three

1. Henrik Ibsen, *The Correspondence of Henrik Ibsen*, ed., Mary Morrison (London, 1905), p. 367.

2. George Bernard Shaw, *The Quintessence of Ibsenism* (London, 1913), pp. 187 - 88.

3. Joseph Wood Krutch, *The Modern Temper* (New York, 1929), p. 8.

4. Allen Tate, *Reactionary Essays on Poetry and Ideas* (New York, 1936), p. 201.

5. Edmund Wilson, "Is Verse a Dying Technique," in *The Triple Thinkers* (New York, 1938), p. 40.

6. Moody's trilogy, *The Masque of Judgement*, is an attempt to "justify the ways of God to man" in the twentieth century through the use of the Prometheus myth. The titles of Mackaye's plays indicate the excessively literary quality of his work: *A Garland to Sylvia, The Canterbury Pilgrims, Sappho and Phaon, Caliban by the Yellow Sands, The Mystery of Hamlet.* Peabody wrote the play *Marlowe* in which the hero quotes his own blank verse.

7. Emerson, "The American Scholar," in Whicher, p. 68.

8. MacLeish's *J.B.* ran for 310 performances on Broadway. Lowell's *The Old Glory* was voted the best off-Broadway. play of 1963. William Alfred's *Hogan's Goat* is another example of a recent verse play which, although written in blank verse, manages to make the old techniques seem new again.

9. *The Fugitive Glory*, in *Man Song* (New York, 1909), p. 73.

10. *The Passing of the Lion*, in *Man Song*, p. 93.

11. *The Passing of the Lion*, p. 96.

12. Grant, 237.

13. *The Death of Agrippina*, in *Lyric and Dramatic Poems*, p. 199.

14. *Agrippina*, p. 216.

15. House, p. 20.

16. "The Alien," in *The Lonesome Trail* (New York, 1907), p. 18.

17. Ibid., p. 29.

18. "The Look in the Face," in *Indian Tales and Others* (New York, 1927), p. 27. All other citations of Neihardt's short stories are from this edition.

19. Elizabeth Drew, *T. S. Eliot: The Design of His Poetry* (London, 1954), p. 22.

20. Emerson, "The Poet," in Whicher, p. 239.

21. Amy C. Rich, review of *The Lonesome Trail* by John G. Neihardt, *The Arena* 38 (August 7, 1907), 22.

22. Anon., "Distinguished Stories," review of *Indian Tales and Others* by John G. Neihardt, New York *Times* October 10, 1926, p. 28.

23. *The Dawn-Builder* (New York, 1911), p. 9. All other citations of *The Dawn-Builder* are from this edition.

24. *Life's Lure* (New York, 1914), pp. 6 - 7. All other citations of *Life's Lure* are from this edition.

25. John T. Flanagan, "John G. Neihardt, Chronicler of the West," *Arizona Quarterly* 21 (Spring, 1965), 18.

26. *When the Tree Flowered* (New York, 1952), pp. 1 - 2. All other citations of *When the Tree Flowered* are from this edition.

27. Paul Engle, review of *When the Tree Flowered* by John G. Neihardt, Chicago *Tribune*, October 7, 1951, p. 5.

28. Oliver LaFarge, review of *When the Tree Flowered* by John G. Neihardt, New York *Herald-Tribune Book Review*, October 7, 1951, p. 16.

Chapter Four

1. R. Brinton, review of *The River and I* by John G. Neihardt, *The Bellman* 10 (June 21, 1911), 68.

2. *The River and I* (New York, 1910), p. 4. All other citations of *The River and I* are from this edition.

3. See Chapter 1, pp. 21 - 23 ff.

4. Mark Twain, *The Adventures of Huckleberry Finn* (New York, 1948), p. 116.

5. Thoreau, *Walden*, in Paul, p. 62.

6. *The Splendid Wayfaring* (New York, 1920), p. viii. All other citations of *The Splendid Wayfaring* are from this edition.

7. *A Cycle of the West* (New York), p. v.

8. The following account is from John G. Neihardt, "The Book That Would Not Die," *Western American Literature* 6 (Winter, 1972), 227 - 30.

9. Ibid., p. 229.

10, John Chamberlain, "A Sioux Indian Tells a Tragic Story," review of *Black Elk Speaks* by John G. Neihardt, New York *Times*, March 6, 1932, p. 4.

11. Sally McKluskey, "*Black Elk Speaks* and So Does John Neihardt," *Western American Literature* 6 (Winter, 1972), 237.

12. Ibid., p. 238.

13. *Black Elk Speaks* (Lincoln, Nebraska, 1961), p. 1. All other citations of *Black Elk Speaks* are from this edition.

Chapter Five

1. Grant, pp. 36 - 37.

2. *The Divine Enchantment* (New York, 1900), p. 5.

3. F. Scott Fitzgerald, *The Great Gatsby* (New York, 1925), p. 119.

4. *The Divine Enchantment*, p. 10.

5. W. E. Black, "Ethic and Metaphysic: A Study of John G. Neihardt," *Western American Literature* 2 (Fall, 1967), 205 - 12.

6. Robert E. Spiller, et al., *A Literary History of the United States* (New York, 1963), p. 165.

7. Frank Norris, *The Octopus* (Boston, 1957), p. 7.

8. Edgeley W. Todd, "The Frontier Epic: Frank Norris and John G. Neihardt," *Western Humanities Review* 13 (Winter, 1959), 151 - 54.

9. Lucy Lockwood Hazard, *The Frontier in American Literature* (New York, 1927), 126 - 37.

10. Kenneth S. Rothwell, "In Search of a Western Epic: Neihardt, Sandburg, and Jaffe as Regionalists and 'Astoriadists,'" *Kansas Quarterly* 2 (Spring, 1970), 57.

11. *The Song of Three Friends*, in *A Cycle of the West* (New York, 1949), pp. 12 - 13. All other citations of *A Cycle of the West* are from this edition.

12. See R. W. B. Lewis, *The American Adam: Tragedy and Tradition in the Nineteenth Century* (Chicago, 1955).

13. Anon., review of *The Song of Three Friends* by John G. Neihardt, *The Dial* 67 (October 4, 1919), 31.

14. William Stanley Braithwaite, review of *The Song of Three Friends*, Boston *Transcript*, March 12, 1919, p. 6.

15. Anon., review of *The Song of Hugh Glass* by John Neihardt, *Yale Review*, cited in *The Splendid Wayfaring*, end papers.

16. *The Splendid Wayfaring*, p. 138.

17. Albert Camus, *The Rebel: An Essay on Man in Revolt* (New York, 1969), p. 23.

18. *All Is But a Beginning*, pp. 48 - 49.

19. "The Ghostly Brother," in *Lyric and Dramatic Poems*, pp. 162 - 64.

20. Anon., review of *The Song of Jed Smith* by John G. Neihardt, *Christian Century* 58 (October 15, 1941), 1274.

21. Maurice Swan, review of *The Song of Jed Smith*, New York *Times*, December 28, 1941, p. 5.

22. See Tony Tanner, *The Reign of Wonder: Naivety and Reality in American Literature* (Cambridge, 1965).

23. Frank Luther Mott, review of *The Song of the Indian Wars* by John G. Neihardt, *The Bookman* 22 (January, 1926), 52.

24. Dee Brown, *Bury My Heart at Wounded Knee* (New York, 1971), p. 130.

25. John T. Flanagan, "John G. Neihardt, Chronicler of the West," *Arizona Quarterly* 21 (Spring, 1965), 14.

26. William Rose Benet, review of *The Song of the Messiah* by John G. Neihardt, *Saturday Review of Literature*, December 7, 1935, p. 46.

Chapter Six

1. *All Is But a Beginning*, p. 170.

2. Leslie A. Fiedler, *The Return of the Vanishing American* (New York, 1968), p. 75.

3. Frank Waters, *The Man Who Killed the Deer* (New York, 1942), p. 311.

4. *All Is But a Beginning*, 172.

5. Ibid.

6. Emerson, *Nature*, in Whicher, p. 24.

Selected Bibliography

PRIMARY SOURCES

1. Books

The Divine Enchantment. New York: J. T. White and Company, 1900.
A Bundle of Myrrh. New York: The Outing Publishing Company, 1907.
The Lonesome Trail. New York: John Lane Company, 1907.
Man Song. New York: Mitchell Kennerly, 1909.
The River and I. New York: G. P. Putnam's Sons, 1910; reprint, Lincoln: University of Nebraska Press, 1968.
The Dawn Builder. New York: Mitchell Kennerly, 1911.
The Stranger at the Gate. New York: Mitchell Kennerly, 1912.
Life's Lure. New York: Mitchell Kennerly, 1914.
The Song of Hugh Glass. New York: The Macmillan Company, 1915.
The Quest. New York: The Macmillan Company, 1916.
The Song of Three Friends. New York: The Macmillan Company, 1919.
The Splendid Wayfaring. New York: The Macmillan Company, 1920; reprint, Lincoln: University of Nebraska Press, 1970.
Two Mothers. New York: The Macmillan Company, 1921.
Laureate Address of John G. Neihardt. Chicago: The Bookfellows, 1921.
The Song of the Indian Wars. New York: The Macmillan Company, 1925.
Poetic Values: Their Reality and Our Need of Them. New York: The Macmillan Company, 1925.
Collected Poems. New York: The Macmillan Company, 1926; reprint, Lincoln: University of Nebraska Press, 1965.
Indian Tales and Others. New York: The Macmillan Company, 1926.
Black Elk Speaks. New York: William Morrow and Company, 1932; reprints, Lincoln: University of Nebraska Press, 1961, and New York: Pocket Books, 1972.
The Song of the Messiah. New York: The Macmillan Company, 1935.
The Song of Jed Smith. New York: The Macmillan Company, 1941.
A Cycle of the West. New York: The Macmillan Company, 1949; reprint, Lincoln: University of Nebraska Press, 1953.

When the Tree Flowered. New York: The Macmillan Company, 1952; reprints, Lincoln: University of Nebraska Press, 1970, and New York: Pocket Books, 1973. Published in England as *Eagle Voice* (London: A. Melrose, 1953).

All Is But a Beginning. New York: Harcourt, Brace, Jovanovich. 1972.

2. Manuscripts and Letters

The John G. Neihardt Papers, which include manuscripts, letters, and other related material, are a part of the Western Historical Manuscripts Collection, University of Missouri Library.

SECONDARY SOURCES

1. Books

HAZARD, LUCY LOCKWOOD, *The Frontier in American Literature.* New York: Thomas Crowell and Company, 1927. Hostile treatment of Neihardt's epics.

HOUSE, JULIUS T. *John G. Neihardt, Man and Poet.* Wayne, Nebraska: F. H. Jones and Company, 1920. Early and perhaps overly enthusiastic appraisal by a close friend of the poet. Useful biographical information.

RICHARDS, JOHN THOMAS. *Luminous Sanity: Literary Criticism Written by John G. Neihardt.* Cape Girardeau, Missouri: Concordia Publishing House, Inc. 1973. Reprints book by House, selected essays, and reviews.

2. Doctoral Dissertations

ALY, LUCILE. "John G. Neihardt as Speaker and Reader." University of Missouri, 1959. Neihardt's oral interpretations of his works.

GRANT, GEORGE PAUL. "The Poetic Development of John G. Neihardt." University of Pittsburgh, 1958. Contains detailed metrical analyses and traces Neihardt's growth in poetic skill.

McCLUSKEY, SALLY. "Image and Idea in the Poetry of John G. Neihardt." Northern Illinois University, 1974. Influence of Neihardt's philosophy on his poetry.

3. Articles

ALY, LUCILE. "The Word-Sender, John G. Neihardt and His Audiences," *Quarterly Journal of Speech* 43 (April, 1957), 151 - 54. Neihardt as platform performer and interpreter of his own work.

BLACK, W. E. "Ethic and Metaphysic: A Study of John G. Neihardt," *Western American Literature* 2 (Fall, 1967), 205 - 12. *The Divine Enchantment* compared with *The Song of the Messiah.*

FLANAGAN, JOHN T. "John G. Neihardt, Chronicle of the West," *Arizona Quarterly* 21 (Spring, 1965), 7 - 20. Good introduction to Neihardt's work.

McCluskey, Sally. "*Black Elk Speaks* and So Does John Neihardt," *Western American Literature* 6 (Winter, 1972), 231 - 42. Literary achievement of Neihardt's best-known work.

Monroe, Harriet. "What of Mr. Neihardt?" *Poetry* 25 (May, 1927), 99 - 104. Important early appraisal.

Rothwell, Kenneth S. "In Search of a Western Epic: Neihardt, Sandburg, and Jaffe as Regionalist and 'Asoriadists,'" *Kansas Quarterly* 2 (Spring, 1970), 53 - 63.

Todd, Edgeley W. "The Frontier Epic: Frank Norris and John G. Neihardt," *Western Humanities Review* 13 (Winter, 1050), 10   15. Neihardt's epic as the fulfillment of Norris's goals.

Index